Building Applications with the Linux Standard Base

ON DEMAND COMPUTING BOOKS

On Demand Computing
Fellenstein

Autonomic Computing
Murch

Grid Computing
Joseph and Fellenstein

Business Intelligence for the Enterprise
Biere

DB2 BOOKS

DB2 Express: Application Development and Deployment
Yip, Cheung, Gartner, Liu, and O'Connell

DB2 Universal Database v8.1 Certification Exam 703 Study Guide
Sanders

The Official Introduction to DB2 for z/OS
Sloan

High Availability Guide to DB2
Eaton and Cialini

DB2 Universal Database v8.1 Certification Exams 701 and 706 Study Guide
Sanders

Integrated Solutions with DB2
Cutlip and Medicke

DB2 Universal Database v8.1 Certification Exam 700 Study Guide
Sanders

DB2 for Solaris: The Official Guide
Bauch and Wilding

DB2 Universal Database v8 Handbook for Windows, UNIX, and Linux
Gunning

Advanced DBA Certification Guide and Reference for DB2 Universal Database v8 for Linux, UNIX, and Windows
Snow and Phan

DB2 Universal Database v8 Application Development Certification Guide, Second Edition
Martineau, Sanyal, Gashyna, and Kyprianou

DB2 Universal Database v8 for Linux, UNIX, and Windows Database Administration Certification Guide, Fifth Edition
Baklarz and Wong

DB2 SQL Procedural Language for Linux, UNIX, and Windows
Yip, Bradstock, Curtis, Gao, Janmohamed, Liu, and McArthur

DB2 Universal Database for OS/390 Version 7.1 Certification Guide
Lawson and Yevich

DB2 Version 8: The Official Guide
Zikopoulos, Baklarz, deRoos, and Melnyk

DB2 UDB for OS/390: An Introduction to DB2 OS/390
Sloan and Hernandez

MORE BOOKS FROM IBM PRESS

The Inventor's Guide to Trademarks and Patents
Fellenstein

WebSphere and Lotus: Implementing Collaboration Solutions
Lamb and Laskey

IBM WebSphere: Deployment and Advanced Configuration
Barcia, Hines, Alcott, and Botzum

IBM WebSphere System Administration
Williamson, Chan, Cundiff, Lauzon, and Mitchell

Developing Quality Technical Information, Second Edition
Hargis, Carey, Hernandez, Hughes, Longo, Rouiller, and Wilde

Enterprise Messaging Using JMS and IBM WebSphere
Yusuf

Enterprise Java Programming with IBM WebSphere, Second Edition

IBM PRESS

Building Applications with the Linux Standard Base

Linux

Written by Core Members of the LSB Team

IBM Press
Pearson plc
Upper Saddle River, NJ • New York • San Francisco
Toronto • London • Munich • Paris • Madrid
Capetown • Sydney • Tokyo • Singapore • Mexico City
www.phptr.com/ibmpress

Library of Congress Cataloging-in-Publication Data

Building applications with the Linux standard base / written by core members of the Linux
 Standard Base Team, George Kraft IV ... [et al.].
  p. cm.
 Includes bibliographical references and index.
 ISBN 0-13-145695-4 (alk. paper)
  1. Linux. 2. Operating systems (Computers) 3. Application software—Development. I.
Kraft, George D., 1937–

QA76.76.O63B8375 2004
005.4'46—dc22

2004054925

Published by Pearson plc
Publishing as IBM Press
Upper Saddle River, New Jersey 07458

Cover design: *IBM Corporation*
IBM Program Managers: *Tara Woodman, Ellice Uffer*
IBM Press Editorial Board: *Richard Ferri*

Printed in the United States of America on recycled paper at Courier in Westford, Massachusetts.

First printing, November 2004

ISBN 0-13-145695-4

Pearson Education LTD.
Pearson Education Australia PTY, Limited
Pearson Education Singapore, Pte. Ltd.
Pearson Education North Asia Ltd.
Pearson Education Canada, Ltd.
Pearson Educación de Mexico, S.A. de C.V.
Pearson Education—Japan
Pearson Education Malaysia, Pte. Ltd.

Contents

Chapter Nine   Adding New Architectures to the LSB Portfolio   113

PART V   USING LSB RESOURCES   119

Chapter Ten   Using the LSB Written Specification   121

Chapter Eleven   Using the LSB Test Suites   129

Foreword

Over the years, there have been many efforts to try to apply standards to the UNIX system and systems sharing its traits. Some of these standards attempted to standardize source-level programming interfaces, such as the Portable Operating System Interface (POSIX) and the Single UNIX Specification (SUS). Others attempted to develop a standard reference implementation trying to unify the operating system utilized by multiple companies—one such example was the Open Software Foundation's OSF/1 operating system.

Unfortunately, past attempts have not been particularly successful in avoiding fragmentation of the marketplace for UNIX systems and providing a single healthy ecosystem upon which software vendors could rely. So why should we believe that Linux Standard Base can succeed where past efforts have not, at least with respect to the needs of independent software vendors (ISVs)?

In order to answer this question, it's necessary to review the history of past standardization efforts for the UNIX system. While they were certainly not all failures, they did not result in the nirvana that ISVs have long been seeking.

Those standards which focused on source-level compatibility, such as POSIX, were critical in the development of a vibrant Open Source community, both before and after that term was coined. Indeed, there is no doubt that Linux owes much of its success to the existence of the POSIX standards. Unfortunately, source-level standards do not provide compatibility at the binary level, and the requirement to support multiple binary images significantly increases the software vendor's support costs. One of the reasons why Java was so enthusiastically adopted by so many people was its promise to allow programmers to *Write (Compile) Once, Run Anywhere*.

One obvious solution which would apparently allow ISVs to ship a single binary image that would work everywhere is to dictate or otherwise standardize on the same operating system or runtime environment. The OSF/1 operating system was one such attempt, but it was a commercial failure. It was adopted by only two companies, neither of which exists today: Kendall Square Research and Digital Equipment Corporation.

At first glance, it would seem that arranging to have multiple competing OS vendors use exactly the same set of software to comprise their runtime environments would solve the compatibility problems that the ISV community has been struggling with. And technically, this would be true. However, there are business, social, and political issues that must be solved.

For example, many decisions that must be made when choosing which features or patches to include in a release are not simple technical questions but involve complicated tradeoffs between support costs, risks of potentially introducing bugs to an otherwise stable platform, versus the benefits of potential increase in sales in particular markets. How these decisions are made by a hardware vendor or a Linux distribution company may be very different depending on their support structure, willingness to take risks, and market focus. So, if one company has 70% of the market, should it have 70% of the decision making power? If not, why would it be willing to surrender the control of its destiny to a dozen of its competitors that together share 30% of the market?

Another problem with mandating a specific implementation is that it is extremely difficult to upgrade the OS software to newer versions without risking breaking application portability. Even security fixes may introduce interoperability problems.

A position midway between a source-level interface standard, such as POSIX, and mandating a specific runtime implementation, such as OSF/1, is to specify an Application Binary Interface (ABI). The Linux Standard Base falls into this camp. The advantage of this approach is that it specifies the minimum necessary to assure true application portability—namely, the binary interfaces. The provider of an LSB Runtime Environment may choose any implementation, so long as it provides the necessary binary interfaces.

In other words, the LSB obeys the old adage, "Do the simplest thing possible, but no simpler." The LSB standardizes what is necessary for binary application compatibility, but does not overconstrain the runtime environment. Indeed, it would be possible for a non-Linux system (such as Solaris or Net/Free/Open BSD) to provide a certified LSB Runtime Environment.

Will the Linux Standard Base succeed? Time will tell, but I believe the current work and momentum bodes well. Recently, the 2.0 version of the Linux Standard Base was released. This version includes full POSIX threads and C++ support. These are the last remaining pieces that will allow software vendors to cost-effectively develop applications that can be used on any LSB Certified Runtime Environment.

When I first started working on the Linux Standard Base, my dream was that someday, ISVs would make software such as personal accounting programs or tax preparation software available under Linux. I believe we are almost at that point. After all, Linux desktop numbers have been growing rapidly, to the point where (depending on which study you believe) Linux is either overtaking or about to overtake another platform for which ISVs have considered it profitable to create such products. And with the Linux Standard Base defining a single platform that ISVs can target, I believe that we will finally start seeing such products—and the LSB will be a large contributor towards this success.

Theodore Ts'o
September, 2004

Preface

WHO SHOULD READ THIS BOOK

This book is intended for anyone who wants to develop LSB-certified Linux applications or work with the LSB workgroup.

Note: Because readers are likely to take different paths through the book, in a small number of cases we have repeated crucial information.

WHAT THE BOOK IS ABOUT

This book outlines the LSB Certification program which takes advantage of the inherent binary compatibility nature of GNU/Linux.

Part I, Introduction, explains the value of standards as well as the difference between source standards and binary standards. It also explains the benefits of certification for application developers, Linux distributions, and end users.

Part II, Developing LSB Applications, covers the important aspects of porting to Linux. This information includes programming differences between Linux and UNIX, packaging software products for any LSB Certified Runtime Environment, and migrating Solaris applications to Linux.

Part III, Certifying for the LSB, outlines the LSB certification procedures for both Linux distributions and software products for those distributions. This information will aid readers wishing to pursue the Free Standard Group's LSB Certification.

Part IV, Contributing to the LSB Project, explains how new interfaces and architectures are added to the LSB Written Specification. Understanding the LSB standardization process is valuable in appreciating the veracity of the LSB and the procedure to follow to expand the scope of the standard.

Part V, Using LSB Resources, outlines how to use the resources provided by the LSB. This information includes a description of the LSB Written Specification, Test Suites, Sample Implementation, Development Environment, and Application Battery. This part also explains how to use and obtain the latest releases of these resources.

Highlighting

The following highlighting conventions are used in this book:

bold   Commands.

`monospace`   Names of files, paths, functions, options, flags, and variables.

`monospace_oblique`   Replaceable elements in a file or path name such as architecture types or provider names.

`$` *`command_line`*   Commands that can be executed as any user (in examples).

`#` *`command_line`*   Commands that should be executed as root (in examples).

`vsx0$` *`command_line`*   Commands that must be executed as user `vsx0`.

`\`   Backslashes are used at the end of long lines in program listing examples to continue to the next line.

Notes are used to identify special commentaries.

About the Authors

Stuart Anderson   Open Source Consultant, netSweng

Stuart Anderson has been involved with Open Source since before the term was created. Stuart is a software engineer and, in the years since 1989, has worked for NCR, AT&T, and Metro Link, Inc., where he has done development work for a wide range of operating systems, from small embedded devices to large multiprocessor servers. Stuart has been involved with the XFree86 project since 1992 and is now a member of the XFree86 core team. Stuart has had previous standards experience with the X Consortium and the System V ABI in the mid '90s, and has been involved with the LSB since its beginning.

Mark Brown   Senior Technical Staff Member, IBM Corporation

Mark Brown has 16 years of UNIX and Linux experience and was release architect for several AIX releases. He specializes in operating system standards specification and implementation, and in binary compatibility issues. He has a B.S. from Texas State University.

Kevin Caunt   Advisory Software Engineer, Linux Technology Center, IBM Systems and Technology Group

Kevin Caunt has more than twenty-five years of computer industry experience and became involved with the Linux Standard Base project in 2000. Since joining, he has been working on various aspects of the

LSB, including test suite development and pilot programs. Kevin is also on the LANANA steering committee. Kevin has been at IBM since 1982, holding various software and hardware engineering positions, and currently works in the Linux Technology Center in Austin, Texas.

Marvin Heffler   Advisory Software Engineer, Linux Technology Center, IBM Systems and Technology Group

Marvin Heffler is a core member of the Linux Standard Base workgroup of the Free Standards Group. This workgroup is driving the effort to standardize parts of the Linux operating system critical to the operation of application programs, thus expanding the scope of application portability. While Marvin has been involved in several areas of the LSB, his main activity has been leading the effort to develop the LSB Application Battery used to validate the proper operation of Linux distributions. Marvin has worked in the IT industry for almost twenty years as a software engineer and software development manager. Marvin graduated in 1984 with a B.S. in computer science from Texas A&M University. Upon graduation Marvin started working for Texas Instruments. Over the next nine years Marvin worked on the development of firmware, SCO Xenix/Unix, and System V.3 for various TI computer systems. In 1993 Marvin joined IBM where he has spent most of his career as a developer and manager for the AIX operating system. Marvin started working on Linux in the summer of 2001 when he joined the IBM Linux Technology Center. In addition to his work on the LSB core team, Marvin works with application development teams within IBM to facilitate adoption of the LSB.

Andrew Josey   Director of Certification, The Open Group

Presently, Andrew Josey chairs the Austin Group, the working group responsible for development of the joint revision to POSIX and the Single UNIX Specification. This work has recently reached International Standard status as ISO/IEC 9945:2003. He is a member of the IEEE Computer Society's Golden Core and is the IEEE P1003.1 Chair and the IEEE PASC Functional Chair of Interpretations.

Andrew is the advocate for Linux and open source within The Open Group. He is the technical lead for the Linux Standard Base testing program, has served as a member of the Board of Directors of the Free Standards Group, and managed the successful development and deployment of the LSB Certification program on behalf of the Free Standards Group.

Andrew has worked in the industry since 1987, working previously for AT&T UNIX Europe, UNIX System Laboratories, and Novell prior to joining The Open Group in 1996.

George Kraft IV   Senior Software Engineer, Linux Technology Center, IBM Systems and Technology Group

George Kraft began working on the LSB as the scribe in October 1999 (LSB v0.1), became the project manager in June 2000 (LSB v0.2), and was elected chairman in March 2001 (LSB v0.7). George served as the chairman and project manager for almost three years. During his tenure, the LSB workgroup released LSB v1.0 (6/01), LSB v1.1 (1/02), LSB v1.2 (6/02), LSB v1.3 (12/02), and LSB v1.9 (8/03), which was a preview of LSB v2.0 (9/04).

As chairman, George coordinated the development of the LSB Written Specification effort, working closely with other LSB team leaders, architects, and team members. George has approximately seventeen years of experience in the IT industry as a UNIX/Linux software engineer. He has been developing on UNIX since 1982, when he began his undergraduate studies at Purdue University in West Lafayette, Indiana, where he earned a B.S. in computer science and mathematics in 1987. He has been developing on Linux since 1993. George has primarily worked in the commands and libraries space in the production of SunOS, BSD, and Dynix for Purdue University, System V.3 for Texas Instruments, AIX 3.x-4.x, and NetBSD 1.4 for IBM. In addition, he worked in the thin client space with Linux for IBM's Network Station (currently under the Netvista brand name). At one time, he was the UNIX team leader for the CAD (Computer Aided Design) Framework Initiative, which was an Electronic Design Automation standards body in Austin, Texas. George's role in IBM's Linux Technology Center was to serve as an advisor within IBM, focusing on how best to integrate the LSB's standards and specifications into IBM's software portfolio.

Scott McNeil   Executive Director, Free Standards Group

Scott McNeil was the cofounder and executive director of the Free Standards Group. Through the efforts of Scott, his team, and numerous contributors, the Free Standards Group has emerged as the leading standards organization for Linux and open source software, with strong support from the international development community, major IT vendors, government agencies, and nonprofit organizations. Since incorporation in 2000, the Free Standards Group has released several versions of its Linux Standard Base (LSB) Written Specification and test suite, and has launched the LSB Certification program, with participation from every major Linux distribution vendor worldwide. In 2003, the Free Standards Group was formally recognized by the Joint Technical Committee of ISO (International Organization for Standardization) and IEC (International Electronical Commission) as a submitter of Publicly Available Specifications (PAS) for Linux— a critical prerequisite for ISO Certification for the Linux operating system.

Under Scott's direction, the Free Standards Group has also managed the OpenI18N workgroup's efforts to develop and deploy internationalization specifications and test suites. Scott was responsible for growing the number of Free Standards Group workgroups to include DWARF, LANANA, OpenPrinting, Open Cluster, and the new Accessibility workgroup.

An active member of the Linux and Open Source community for over eight years, Scott has previously held management positions at companies such as VA Linux and SuSE and is currently working at IBM.

Kristin Thomas   Information Developer, IBM Systems and Technology Group

Kristin Thomas is an information developer supporting the AIX operating system. Before working on AIX, Kristin wrote Linux documentation in IBM's Linux Technology Center. In the Linux Technology Center, she wrote documentation for open source projects, such as the Linux Standard Base, openCryptoki, and the IBM

Carrier Grade Open Framework reference implementation. Kristin has been with IBM since 2000, writing documentation for IBM's Software Group and Systems and Technology Group. She is a 2000 graduate of the Masters of Arts in Technical Communication program at Texas Tech University.

Radhakrishnan Sethuraman   Software Engineer, Linux Integration Center, IBM Software Group

Radhakrishnan Sethuraman is a solutions engineer who works as part of the solutions division of Linux Integration Center (LIC). As a solutions engineer he worked on various telco initiatives of the LIC. He currently works in the retail initiative (ROLO). In these roles, he has been working with IBM middleware such as WebSphere, DB2, MQ, and Tivoli, running mainly on Linux. He graduated in 2002 with an M.S. in computer science at Texas Tech University. He has been with IBM since 2002.

Matt Taggart   Free Software Engineer, Linux and Open Source Lab, Hewlett-Packard

Matt Taggart is a founding member of HP's Linux and Open Source Lab where he works on Linux OS development. Matt joined HP in 1996 and has also worked in the HP-UX Workstation Division. He has been using Linux since 1994 and became involved with the Linux Standard Base project in 2001 by coordinating the LSB Futures subcommittee and helping out with project infrastructure. In addition to his work at HP, Matt is a developer with the Debian project and coordinates LSB compliance for the project. He received a B.S. in chemical and environmental engineering from Colorado State University in 1996 and currently lives in Seattle, Washington.

Theodore Ts'o   STSM, Linux Technology Center, IBM Systems and Technology Group

Theodore Ts'o has served on the board of the Free Standards Group (FSG) since its founding, bringing his experience of standards development from the Internet Engineering Task Force to the FSG. Within the IETF, he serves on the Security Area Directorate, and as a chair of the IPSEC working group. Within the FSG, Theodore has contributed to the Linux Standard Base and served as a board member. Theodore also organizes the annual Linux Kernel Developers workshop (and is a kernel developer himself). He has also served on several Usenix conference program committees, including chairing the program committee for the Atlanta Linux Showcase in 2000.

Mats Wichmann   Linux Standards Architect, Software Solutions Group, Intel Corporation

Mats Wichmann has been a developer with the LSB project since 2001, and was elected LSB chairman in January 2004. Within the LSB, he participates in the LSB Steering Committee, the Specification Authority, and works with all the LSB subgroups. He is also the lead developer for the LSB Sample Implementation. Mats has been a UNIX and, later, Linux developer since 1980 and has also worked as a consultant, trainer, and courseware developer. He has past standards and ABI experience with the MIPS ABI Group where he worked as technical director. He is a member of the Austin Group and the IEEE Standards Association.

Christopher Yeoh   Software Engineer, Linux Technology Center, IBM Systems and Technology Group

Christopher Yeoh has been using Linux since 1994 and became involved with the Linux Standard Base project in 2000. Since joining, he has been working on various aspects of the LSB, including test suite development and the LSB Development Environment. Christopher is currently acting as the technical lead for the LSB Development Environment. He is an employee of the IBM Linux Technology Center, working at OzLabs in Canberra, Australia. Previously, he worked on the design and development of multidimensional graphical visualization and GIS products with real-time capabilities.

## PART I

Introduction

Linux Standard Base (LSB) is a term that is used to describe both an organization and a standard. Since its inception in 1998, the LSB project has been supported by countless participants interested in developing a standard to unify and bolster the operability of Linux. Their cooperative effort has resulted in the releasing of multiple products that are calculated to establish Linux as a viable and affordable platform with broad market potential.

Within the Linux community, the credibility of the LSB project is a factor of the legitimacy of the LSB standard. This part provides background information about the LSB organization.

Chapter 1 discusses the background and basic principles behind the LSB. It also explains the structure of the organization and the value of standards. Chapter 2 introduces the concept of binary compatibility. It explains the importance of binary compatibility and how to achieve it in your applications.

## CHAPTER ONE

Understanding the LSB

This chapter describes the Linux Standard Base, giving an overview of its evolution from the concept to the Linux Standard Base 2.0 edition. It describes the benefits of the specification, provides a brief history of the work that led to its creation, and places the specification in context with other industry standards initiatives.

The Linux Standard Base (LSB) Written Specification is an application binary interface standard for shrink-wrapped applications. The LSB draws on the source standards of the IEEE POSIX standards and The Open Group's Single UNIX Specification for many of its behavioral interface definitions. Some interfaces are not included in the LSB, since they are outside the remit of a binary runtime environment; typically these are development interfaces or user-level tools. The LSB also extends the source standards in other areas (such as graphics) and includes the necessary details such as the binary execution file formats to support a high volume binary application platform.

1.1 BACKGROUND

Today, the cost of developing application software is considerably greater than the cost of the hardware on which the applications run. Preserving this investment in critical applications of an organization, while allowing the organization to freely mix and match platforms as hardware costs fall, has led to the idea of open systems. One of the cornerstones of open systems is portability—the ability to move the source code of an application to another platform and rebuild the application without changing the source.

Software portability problems do not just affect an organization directly through that organization's own applications. Hardware vendors often find their market limited by the applications that run on their platforms. Independent software vendors (ISVs) often limit themselves in the number of platforms on which they sell their products, due to the costs of maintaining ports of the application for multiple platforms. Consumers are caught, often choosing hardware platforms based on the applications they need to purchase, but without the ability to know what new applications will be available on these platforms in the future.

Whilst open systems have allowed source portability, source portability is not the solution for creating a large consumer market; for that, binary portability is a must. The LSB Written Specification provides an open consensus specification to support development of portable binary shrink-wrapped applications for the Linux platform. The stated goals of the LSB are "to develop and promote a set of standards that will increase compatibility," the key differentiator being that LSB's approach is at the binary interface level.

1.2   THE VALUE OF STANDARDS

The increasing popularity of the Linux operating system has spawned a large number of distributions with variations in the features they deliver. This could, if left unattended, lead to unnecessary fragmentation of Linux. Standardization of a Linux binary platform for volume applications is both desirable and attainable, and a large value can be attained if the "bar of commonality," that is, the standard, is raised to a sufficient level. There is often much more to be gained by having key functionality share a common interface and/or behave in exactly the same way, than for it to be different. In this context, the LSB has built on the work of many existing standards and specifications and thus is raising the commonality level. This is the value of standards.

1.3   THE FREE STANDARDS GROUP

The Free Standards Group (FSG)[1] is the industry's first independent, non-profit organization dedicated to accelerating the use and acceptance of open source technologies through the development, application, and promotion of standards. The FSG delivers access to standards, tools, and compliance testing, which allows open source developers to concentrate on adding value to Linux, without spending time dealing with verification and porting issues. Key projects that fall under the FSG umbrella include the Linux Standard Base (LSB) and OpenI18N (Open Internationalization).[2]

1.4   ORGANIZATIONAL STRUCTURE OF THE LSB

The LSB workgroup is led by an elected chair and governed by a Steering Committee. Figure 1.1 shows the structure of the organization as a whole.

The following list describes the roles of its workgroup members.

1.4.1   Chair

The LSB chair is the overall project lead. The chair coordinates all projects and represents the LSB to the Free Standards Group (FSG) and to the community. The chair is elected by the LSB contributors of the LSB workgroup and has a term of office of two years. The chair can be removed through a majority vote of no confidence by either the Steering Committee or the Free Standards Group board of directors. The chair has the following responsibilities and duties:

- Overseeing the production and dissemination of the roadmap, budget, media, and collaboration

- Conducting a workgroup telephone conference at least once per month

- Conducting a face-to-face workgroup meeting at least once per year but not more than twice

---

1. http://www.freestandards.org/

2. http://www.openi18n.org/

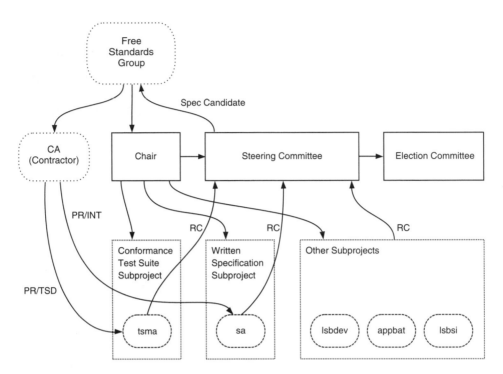

Figure 1.1: LSB Organizational Structure

- Presenting a roadmap and budget to the workgroup and FSG board once per year
- Acting as the primary spokesperson for the LSB workgroup
- Nominating a project manager, a release manager, and subproject team leaders

1.4.2   Election Committee

The Election Committee is an ad hoc committee of LSB contributors, who are appointed by the Steering Committee to elect a new chair when the chair position becomes vacant or the term of office expires. The committee shall have two to six members and is responsible for selecting one or more candidates for chair at least 30 days in advance of the election date.

1.4.3 Steering Committee

The LSB Steering Committee includes the chair and the subproject team leaders, as well as any other LSB contributor the chair feels strongly should be on the committee. Any of the LSB Steering Committee members may represent the LSB as a spokesperson. Steering Committee members may serve indefinitely as long as they are actively conducting business in the best interest of the LSB. Steering Committee members may be removed on a majority vote of no confidence by the Steering Committee. An individual may serve as team lead for more than one subproject, but this shall in no event entitle him or her to more than a single vote on the steering committee. The Steering Committee shall have a minimum of three members; if there are not sufficient team leaders then the chair shall solicit a general member of the LSB workgroup to fill out the Steering Committee. A majority vote from the LSB Steering Committee is required to commence or conclude work (such as draft specifications) or make resolutions. A quorum of 50% of the sitting members of the Steering Committee is required for a valid vote. No interest group (for example, company or organization) may cast a majority of the votes.

1.4.4 Project Manager/Release Manager

The LSB chair can appoint a project manager and/or release manager to manage an LSB release of the Written Specification and certification materials. The project manager or release manager position does not confer a Steering Committee seat.

1.5 LSB SPECIFICATION OVERVIEW

The LSB is composed of two basic parts: a common specification ("generic LSB" or "gLSB") describing those parts of the interface that remain constant across all implementations of the LSB, and an architecture-specific specification ("archLSB") describing the parts of the interface that vary by processor architecture. Together, the generic LSB and the architecture-specific supplement for a single hardware architecture provide a complete interface specification for compiled application programs on systems that share a common hardware architecture.

The architecture-specific supplement must be used in conjunction with the generic LSB. It provides architecture-specific information that supplements the generic LSB, as well as additional information that is not found in the generic LSB.

For an in depth description, see Chapter 10.

1.6   BENEFITS FOR APPLICATION DEVELOPERS

A standard application binary interface for Linux provides increased confidence in your application, reduced expenses, and enhanced market opportunities.

1.6.1   Increasing Confidence in Your Application

The widespread success of a software application is heavily dependent on customers' confidence in the application. Instilling confidence depends on several factors, including compatibility, portability, and reliability. Compatibility is rapidly becoming a requirement for customers who need applications that run with a wide variety of other applications. Customers are also demanding that applications be written for maximum portability. Customers run applications in many different environments that may include different operating systems and different architectures, and they do not want to purchase a different version of an application for each environment. Reliability is also an important requirement for customers today. Software applications run everything from bank transactions to hospital information systems, so customers can not afford to use unreliable applications.

LSB Certification provides the independent assurance that an application will meet customers' compatibility, portability, and reliability expectations. Since the LSB allows you to standardize your software, LSB Certification assures its compatibility among Linux distributions. Compliance with the LSB also ensures that your software applications will run on any compliant system, increasing your and your customers' confidence to use Linux across architectures and with other applications. The extensive set of LSB Test Suites also gives you the tools to prove your applications' reliability to customers.

1.6.2   Reducing Expenses

Reducing expenses is always an important goal in any business, and there are many expense reducing measures that can be introduced into the development process. Relying on a common base of *application programming interfaces* (APIs) can greatly reduce the need to develop new code when you develop an application. Using common APIs also reduces the expenses involved in adding support for additional operating systems. You can also lower expenses by testing your application in only one operating environment. If the application runs the same way in all compatible operating environments, then your test effort can be much smaller. You can also reduce expenses by relying on a common set of preexisting test cases. Using common test cases lessens the time and resources involved in testing. With less time and resources needed to migrate and test your application, you can focus on product innovation instead of the bottom line.

Instead of duplicating product testing on each operating system support-ed, you only have to fully test the application once. Software that can run on any Linux system without change eliminates dependencies specific to various Linux distributions. The value proposition of using the LSB on Linux is to be binary compatible, which enables reduced test expenses in the ever growing Linux domain. With the LSB, ISVs are able to channel their resources into product innovation instead of spending excessive time on maintenance.

1.6.3   Enhancing Market Opportunities

Increasing confidence in your applications and reducing the expenses involved in developing them can greatly enhance your market opportunities. Normally, limited resources can restrict a product to a certain niche market. However, increased confidence and reduced expenses can open up previously unavail-able market opportunities. For example, when the need to support all the possible combinations of operating systems and computer hardware is elimi-nated, the opportunities for an application are expanded with minimum effort. Instead of creating custom versions of the application for different op-erating environments, you can produce a shrink-wrapped version with the capability to be used in multiple environments. The shrink-wrapped applica-tion can help you quickly meet the needs of new and changing market opportunities.

The Linux Standard Base is the tool you can use today to expand the market reach of your products. The choice of target Linux systems for your applications meets the diverse requirements of your customers. Interchangeable Linux systems enhance market opportunities for your software applications on Linux.

1.7   BENEFITS FOR USERS

The Linux Standard Base ensures a standardized binary application platform for Linux available from multiple suppliers, which gives users freedom of choice without being locked into a single supplier's offerings. It also offers the prospect of a supply of applications that can run across a range of systems from multiple suppliers.

1.8   BENEFITS FOR DISTRIBUTIONS

Differentiating the core competence of the operating system is contrary to a ubiquitous Linux application runtime environment. Independent software vendors desire the stability and compatibility of Linux. The LSB gives a precise definition and an easy validation process. Distributions can succinctly provide compatible core libraries and commands, which affords the distributions more time to spend on other areas for their customers.

1.9   BRIEF HISTORY OF THE LSB PROJECT

The Linux Standard Base (LSB) project was first announced in May 1998 with a project proposal and call for participation.[3] The announcement included the endorsement of Linus Torvalds, Bruce Perens, Eric Raymond, several Linux distributors, ISVs, members of Linux International, as well as Jordan Hubbard of the FreeBSD project. At that time, the stated aim of the project was to provide a "vendor-neutral standard, backed by source code, upon which to build Linux distributions," including a reference platform. The

---

3. http://old.lwn.net/1998/0528/a/lsb.html

stated result of the project would be that any program that ran successfully on the reference platform would be expected to run on all Linux systems that are in compliance with the standard.

The project deliverables have changed since the original proposal and are now structured to provide a set of specifications and test tools in addition to the reference implementation (which is now called the Sample Implementation). There is also an Application Battery which is a set of real-world LSB-conformant applications used to test the specification and runtimes.

Since May 2000, the legal framework under which the LSB project operates is a workgroup of the Free Standards Group. The Free Standards Group is an independent nonprofit organization dedicated to accelerating the use and acceptance of open source technologies through the development, application, and promotion of standards.

The first official version of the LSB Written Specification was released in June 2001. Since then there have been regular updates to the specification released at approximately six month intervals. The first version of the specification only supported the Intel IA32 (386 and above) architecture, with additional architectures being added in later updates. Currently, the specification supports the following architectures:

- IA32
- 32-bit PowerPC
- Itanium
- 64-bit PowerPC
- 31-bit S390
- 64-bit z/Architecture

In parallel with the LSB Written Specification, a set of test tools have been developed for testing compliance to the LSB for runtime environments and applications. The first general release of the test tools was made in December 2001. With the release of the LSB 1.2 Written Specification and its associated test tools in August 2002, the Free Standards Group introduced the LSB Certification program. Only suppliers of certified products may use the LSB trademark in connection with their product. Many of the most prominent Linux distributions have been certified. LSB 2.0, which was released in 2004, includes C++, C99, SUSv3, NPTL, and IPv6.

## CHAPTER TWO

Ensuring
Binary Compatibility

Binary compatibility is a feature assurance given by an LSB Certified Runtime Environment to an application. You can take advantage of that assurance by using the LSB as guidance when coding your application. This is part of the promise and value of the Linux Standard Base. This chapter explains the concept of binary compatibility and its importance in developing LSB-certified applications. It also describes each step in the process of ensuring binary compatibility and discusses the different source code standards the LSB Written Specification adheres to. Finally, there is a discussion of binary versus source code compatibility.

2.1   ILLUSTRATION OF BINARY COMPATIBILITY

Linux inherently has binary compatibility. Without the need to rebuild or port source code from one Linux release or distribution to another, Linux has achieved binary compatibility for a given hardware platform. You only have to build once for each Linux architecture, such as IA32, PowerPC, or Itanium, and then deploy. The LSB has set some rules and guidelines that make this feature practical for applications. The path to shrink-wrapping an LSB application for Linux includes the following steps:

- Coding to the portability layer
- Using the correct ABIs
- Testing with the LSB application checker

- Following the LSB packaging guidelines
- Seeking LSB certification

The following sections describe each of these steps in detail.[1]

2.1.1   Coding to the Portability Layer

Rather than let applications access operating system resources directly, open systems such as UNIX and Linux have a portability layer for applications to be coded to. For UNIX, this coding layer is the set of POSIX application programming interfaces (APIs). However, since we know that "GNU's Not UNIX," the LSB has referenced POSIX for Linux in the form of the LSB Written Specification standard (Figure 2.1).

Applications must not use private interfaces of the operating system, or subvert the portability layer by accessing operating system resources directly. Some applications access system resources directly in order to be *platform-tuned*. Platform-tuning of an application may increase performance, but it greatly diminishes the possibility that the software will be binary compatible between systems or releases. This kind of software is sometimes platform-branded to work for a particular release of an operating system, which is fine

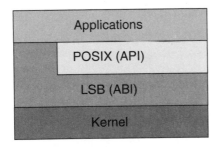

Figure 2.1: LSB Layer

---

1. Portions of this chapter were derived with permission from "Five steps to binary-compatible Linux applications" by George Kraft IV, IBM DeveloperWorks, October 2002 (`http://www.ibm.com/developerworks/linux/library/l-lsb.html`).

if that is the intent. This style of programming, however, is outside the scope of the LSB.

Applications that are coded to the LSB Written Specification have taken the first step to becoming binary compatible among the set of LSB-branded systems. By coding to the specification, the application is limited to using only the following system libraries: **libc**, **libdl**, **libm**, **libutil**, **libcrypt**, **libz**, **libpthread**, **libncurses**, **libX11**, **libXext**, **LibXt**, **libICE**, **libSM**, and **libGL**.

If an application cannot limit itself to the interfaces of the libraries previously listed, then—to minimize runtime errors—the application must either bundle the nonspecified library as part of the application, or it must statically link the library to the application. However, the libraries themselves must be LSB-compliant by using only the interfaces of the libraries listed in the previous paragraph.

2.1.2   Using the Correct ABIs

Restricting your development to the source API specification is not enough for binary compatibility because different releases and different systems have different versions of the libraries. To become binary compatible, you must develop to the ABI. Linux has the ability to version individual ABIs. So, if an imaginary function, myfunction(x,y), currently returns a double, but a more recent version of the ABI returns an integer, then you must use the version that was specified to return the original data type. To help you do this, the LSB has created stub libraries. You can link to the LSB stub libraries and to the LSB runtime linker. Then the LSB-specified ABI alone can be used. Either the application build will get an unresolved symbol error because it was using something not specified by the LSB, or the LSB stub libraries will ensure the correct ABIs per the binary specification.

To simplify the compilation of an application with the correct ABIs, the LSB provides an **lsbcc** wrapper script. This script uses the LSB stub libraries with the correct ABIs, the LSB runtime linker (ld-lsb.so.2), and header files corresponding to the LSB Written Specification. You can download the lsb-build-base and lsb-build-cc packages, and then integrate them into your normal build procedure.

2.1.3   Testing with the LSB Application Checker

The LSB application checker, **lsbappchk**, is a test tool that checks applications for LSB ABI compliance. The **lsbappchk** tool compares the ABI symbols used by an application to ABI symbols defined by the LSB Written Specification. Example 2.1 shows a "Hello World" application that uses the `getpid()` API.

Example 2.1: "Hello World"

```
#include <stdio.h>
#include <unistd.h>

main()
{
    printf("hello world: %d\n", getpid());
}
```

Once compiled, you can check `helloworld.c` to determine if it is LSB-compliant (Example 2.2).

Example 2.2: Checking for LSB Compliance

```
$ lsbcc -o hw_good helloworld.c

$ lsbappchk hw_good
lsbappchk for LSB Specification 2.0
Checking binary hw_good
```

We see from the **lsbappchk** output that it did not find any compliance anomalies. However, if we slightly change the previous example to use the private function `_getpid()`, we see different results (Example 2.3).

Example 2.3: Using the `_getpid()` Function

```
$ lsbcc -o hw_bad helloworld.c
/tmp/cc5CITzio.o: In function 'main':
/tmp/cc5CITzio.o(.text_0xd): undefined reference to '_getpid'
collect2: ld returned 1 exit status
```

From the standard error (stderr) output of **lsbcc**, we can see that **lsbcc** would not compile the application with a noncompliant ABI. Using the LSB **lsbcc** tool helps you avoid creating noncompliant applications. But what if we used the native compiler?

Example 2.4: Native Compiler

```
$ cc -o hw_bad helloworld.c
```

The native compiler (Example 2.4) allows the application to link with the private interface _getpid() of the system, but we know from the LSB Written Specification that this is wrong. In addition, we know that we should never use any interface that is prefixed with an underscore.

From the **lsbappchk** stderr output in Example 2.5, we can see the application uses a wrong runtime loader and the noncompliant _getpid() ABI. So, even if you do not use **lsbcc** to catch nonconformance issues, you can still use **lsbappchk** later to validate the application. This methodology is not bulletproof, but it is a good indicator.

Example 2.5: **lsbappchk** Stderr Output

```
$ lsbappchk hw_bad
lsbappchk for LSB Specification 2.0
Checking binary hw_bad
Incorrect program interpreter: /lib/ld-linux.so.2
Symbol _getpid used, but not part of LSB
```

2.1.4 Following LSB Packaging Guidelines

Once your application is built using the LSB headers and linked with the LSB stub libraries and runtime loader, you can start packaging your application the LSB way. The LSB suggests that you package your application in the RPM format as specified by the LSB Written Specification. In addition, you may not use triggers, nor depend on the execution order of preinstall or preuninstall scripts. You are also limited to using only the commands specified by the LSB in those scripts and in your application, because other commands are not guaranteed to be present or to behave in expected ways. The LSB does not specify the tool to install these RPM-packaged applications. You can use the **rpm** tool on RPM-based systems, and **alien** on Debian. For more information on packaging, see Chapter 4.

In addition to avoiding namespace collisions in the filesystem hierarchy, LSB-conforming packages are prefixed with `lsb-`. If the name of the package only contains one hyphen, this name must be registered with LANANA. If the package name contains more than one hyphen, then the area between the first pair of hyphens must be either an LSB provider name registered with LANANA, or your fully-qualified domain name in lowercase. For example, `lsb-java` may be a name registered with LANANA by Sun Microsystems, but there may be another Java package name, `lsb-unregistered.org-java`, which does not need to be registered. For more information on LANANA, see Section 4.3.

2.1.5   Seeking LSB Certification

The last step in developing an LSB application is getting certified. Any LSB-certified application can run on any LSB-certified distribution. Today, there are dozens of certified distributions, and the LSB has built example conforming open source applications.

To get LSB certification, you will complete the following steps:

- Register yourself on the LSB Certification Web site.
- Self-test your application using the LSB-provided tests, and then upload the results.
- Warrant that the application passes your own FVT.
- Complete the Conformance Statement Questionnaire.
- Sign the LSB Trademark License Agreement.
- Receive confirmation from the Certification Authority.
- Pay the certification fees and sign the LSB Certification Agreement.

The LSB trademark can only be used by LSB-certified applications; no other statement of compliance can be made. For more information, see Section 7.2.

2.2   SOURCE CODE STANDARDS

The standardization of a set of Application Programming Interfaces (APIs) for the purpose of recompile compatibility between systems is a source code standard.

2.2.1   POSIX

The Institute of Electrical and Electronics Engineers (IEEE) is the group that has developed and continues to develop the POSIX family of standards. Beginning in the mid-1980s, this group picked up on the work already done by the UNIX user organization UniForum (the 1984 /usr/group Standard) and began to produce an operating system standard under Project 1003 (POSIX).

The best known POSIX document is IEEE Std 1003.1 (also known as POSIX 1003.1), but the term "POSIX" actually covers a set of related operating system specifications. The various subprojects instituted under 1003 are staffed by individual volunteers representing a cross-section of skills such as hardware manufacturing, OS development, software and tools development, academia, governments, and more.

The name POSIX was suggested by Richard Stallman, one of the participants. It is pronounced pahz-icks, as in positive.

As stated in the cover material for these standards, there were several principles guiding their development, the key ones being application source portability, specification of the interface without requiring a particular implementation, and reliance on historical practice.

Another goal is *consensus*. There are some features of historical (and modern) UNIX-based operating systems which are not found in POSIX, because no consensus could be reached at the time work was being done. This is the reason there is no mention of either **tar** or **cpio** in the 1003.2 specification, for example. Where there was no consensus, the feature was left out to produce a specification with a high enough level of approval to pass the IEEE voting rules: at least a 75% return on ballots; no more than 30% of eligible balloters abstaining; at least 75% "yes" votes.

More information about the Portable Application Standards Committee (PASC), the guiding body for IEEE POSIX, is available online.[2]

2.2.1.1   POSIX 1003.1 System Application Interface (C API)

Together with 1003.2 (discussed in Section 2.2.1.2), 1003.1 is the base upon which the POSIX family of standards has been built. This is the "API and header files" part of the pair, the other being the "shell and utilities." In keeping with its original focus on the UNIX system, it is aimed at interactive timesharing computing environments.

POSIX 1003.1 was first published in 1988. A revised edition was published in 1990. The 1990 edition became an international standard, ISO/IEC 9945–1:1990.

In 1996, a new edition was created, which added realtime and threads features as optional extension sets to the base 1990 standard. This also became an international standard, ISO/IEC 9945–1:1996. After that, other optional feature sets were created, but remained separate documents (called *amendments* to the base 1990 standard) until 1999.

A major revision of the core standard, approved in 1998, rolled up the various amendments, options, and interpretations. The proposal also merged 1003.1 with 1003.2 to create one document encompassing the OS space. The result is known as IEEE POSIX 1003.1–2001, comprised of four volumes totaling 3,760 pages.

2.2.1.2   POSIX 1003.2 Shell and Utilities

This specification defines a portable shell scripting environment (the so-called *POSIX shell*) and a base set of portable utilities. In some places, where there was no consensus on the current tools (and a definite need was shown), a new tool was invented. The **pax** archive tool is an example of this.

---

2. http://www.pasc.org/

The emphasis is again on defining things required to make applications portable. There is a section on the preferred syntax for new utilities' arguments and options. In some cases *user portability* was considered, such as the inclusion of the **vi** editor.

2.2.2 Single UNIX Specification

The Single UNIX Specification (SUS) is a set of specifications required for UNIX trademark compliance. It is developed and managed by The Open Group, an industry consortium and marketing group. The Open Group establishes the definition of what a UNIX system is and holds its associated trademark in trust for the industry. The SUS specifies the programming and user environment that must be offered by an operating system before the system can use the UNIX trademark.

Version 3 of the Single UNIX Specification is the latest in the series of UNIX specifications that began with the X/Open Company Portability Guides (XPGs), which were operating system specifications created prior to, and then concurrently with, the initial POSIX efforts. In late 1998, The Open Group, IEEE, and ISO/IEC SC22/WG15 agreed to work together to form a single common set of specifications with the development group known as the Austin Group (described later in this section).

The Single UNIX Specification has always been aligned with the formal API standards such as POSIX and ISO C, being an upward compatible superset. It contains more APIs and features than POSIX, and it makes mandatory some features that POSIX keeps optional. POSIX threads, for example, are required for UNIX trademark compliance. The SUS also covers X11, Curses, and many more mandatory utilities than POSIX.

An HTML version of the specification is freely available from The Open Group's Single UNIX Specification Web site.[3]

---

3. http://www.unix.org/version3/

More information about the SUS[4] and the Open Group[5] can be found online on their respective Web sites.

2.2.2.1   The Austin Group

"The Austin Group" is the name given to a joint working group created by the IEEE, ISO, and The Open Group in September 1998. These specification bodies agreed that the best thing for OS implementors and application developers was to have one set of documents that contained the text of the POSIX, ISO, and SUS specifications. In this way, conflicts and confusion between the standards, as well as the work needed to maintain the various documents, could be reduced.

This body consists of individual volunteers, including members of the Free Software and Open Source communities. The group is chaired by the ISO project editor, and the founding bodies (IEEE, ISO, and Open Group) each have one organizational representative. The ORs hold controlling votes, which are only used when issues without a clear consensus require a vote. IEEE and The Open Group hold joint copyright over the resulting work.

The Austin Group is the actual technical body that produced the standard known variously as IEEE POSIX 1003.1–2001, the Single UNIX Specification Version 3, and ISO/IEC 9945:2002.

Information on the Austin Group is available from its Web site.[6]

2.3   BINARY STANDARDS

In the past there have been many binary standards such as *System V Application Binary Interface* for the MIPS RISC processor, *88open* for the Motorola 88000 RISC processor, and *PowerOpen Environment* for the PowerPC processor; however, none have been as successful as the *Linux Standard Base*. The LSB ensures that an LSB-certified application complied for a particular family

---

4. http://www.unix-systems.org/

5. http://www.opengroup.org/

6. http://www.opengroup.org/austin/

of processors can run on any corresponding LSB Certified Runtime
Environment.

2.4   LSB BINARY COMPATIBILITY

Binary compatibility is the expectation that a properly-coded application,
which executes successfully and correctly on one instantiation of an operating
system, will continue to do so on another OS of the same hardware platform.
The LSB is dedicated to the idea that Linux-based applications can be portable
across Linux operating system distributions. Now that a specification exists
that both operating system providers and application developers can agree
upon, users are already benefiting from increased compatibility of their
applications and tools.

2.4.1   Binary versus Source Compatibility

Binary compatibility is not the same as source compatibility. A source code
fragment that describes the same operation on two instances of an OS can
become a binary that will only operate on one of them, even on the same
hardware platform. Binary compatibility is a "contract" between the OS and
the application; the OS will provide a set of known functions in a specified
way, and the application will use those functions and avoid other functions
for which there is no specification.

   The LSB provides this contract. For the OS, it describes both the set of
known functions and the known way of making them available. It does this
via its programming interface (API) and binary interface (ABI) documents
for each hardware platform. For applications, the LSB offers testing and certification to assure that only the functions provided for by the LSB are used.

2.4.2   Coding Compatible Applications

Applications using only the LSB-documented interfaces will run unmodified
on all LSB-certified OSes for a given hardware architecture family, as described
by that LSB ABI specification architecture. Application software that meets
this specification and successfully passes testing using the LSB Application

certification process can be considered portable on all members of that architecture.

This means that the application uses no undocumented interfaces, as well as has no dependencies on specific types of hardware (for example, specific mass storage devices or specific I/O or networking adapters). This also means that only LSB-certified OSes for that architecture can be relied upon as a base for the application.

2.4.3   Looking Forward

Applications that are LSB-certified are binary compatible within an LSB release set. The LSB does not support application compatibility between major releases. However, it may be possible for a Linux distribution to conform to multiple versions of the LSB at the same time.

2.4.4   Value Proposition

In the past, the benefits of *source code portability* between variants of UNIXes and hardware platforms were well established. Today, there is no larger success demonstrating *binary compatibility* than Linux as specified by the LSB. Software development evolving from source code portability to binary compatibility is dramatically increasing product reliability in this multivendor Linux market. It enables the redirection of the time spent on porting and testing to product innovation.

2.4.5   Shrink-Wrapped Applications

Linux software that is LSB-certified to be binary compatible can be shrink-wrapped and sold in retail stores with a longer shelf life and wider customer base. Dependencies on specific releases of certain Linux systems are obsolete.

## PART II

Developing LSB Applications

Linux distributions' conformance to standard ABIs and ELF is all about providing runtime environment stability and consistency for applications; however, operating system robustness is only half the equation for true compatibility. In addition to having an LSB Certified Runtime Environment, one needs competent Linux applications. Well-behaved applications that are generically Linux-compatible need to strictly use the prescribed public APIs and commands, generically package, and follow the FHS filesystem layout.

## CHAPTER THREE

Using LSB Coding Practices

This chapter describes the coding practices you should use to develop LSB-certified applications. It gives overviews and examples of many of the *do's* and *don'ts* of LSB coding practices. Each section includes an explanation of the concept and a code example of that concept.

3.1 C AND C++

This chapter assumes the reader is a knowledgeable C, UNIX, or Linux programmer. Suggested prerequisite readings might be: *Practical C Programming*, *Understanding UNIX/Linux Programming*, *Programming with GNU Software*, or *Learning the bash Shell*.

The LSB references both the "ISO/IEC 9899: 1999, Programming Languages—C" and "ISO/IEC 14882: 1998(E) Programming Languages—C++" for C and C++ programming, respectively. The GNU Compiler Collection (GCC) project has implemented these ISO/IEC standards and is monitoring compliance status. Developers should feel confident about this crucial element of open source development.

3.2   INTERNATIONALIZATION

It is good to strive to write reusable and portable code; however, sometimes the usefulness of the software has inadvertent limits because the language and cultural requirements of the end user are not actively considered. Fortunately, these issues are well understood and the solution has been put in place by the GNU Translation project. Linux provides the capability to extract culturally dependent data from the application (internationalization) and apply it to various cultures as desired (localization).

Take for example a simple "Hello World" program that prints a short text message on the screen. Will the message be displayed in English, Spanish, Japanese, or Jamaican English? This depends on whether the original text has been translated and properly stored in a message catalog for the application to use, and on whether the end user has set his or her locale to find those messages. The `setlocale()` function in Example 3.1 can initialize the locale based on the first nonempty value of the three environment variables `LC_ALL`, `LC_MESSAGES`, or `LANG`.

If the end user sets `LANG` to `en_US` then the program will look for U.S. English translated text found in the `ghw` message catalog in the `/usr/share/locale/` directory set by `bindtextdomain()`.

Instead of printing a text message directly using `printf()`, the `gettext()` function is called to look up the `MSGID` (the default text) in the current default message catalog for the current `LC_MESSAGES` locale. If it's not found, the function returns `MSGID` itself (the default text).

Beware that Linux has added `gettext()` even though POSIX defines `catgets()` that is used on UNIX. The difference between these methods is that `catgets()` uses a numeric message identifier, whereas `gettext()` uses the default text as the message identifier. The disadvantage of `catgets()` is that the numeric message identifiers can easily get out of sync between the application and the message catalog. The text message identifiers of `gettext()` at least have a chance of being found in the message catalog if they were moved out of sequence but not altered. For obvious reasons, never try to use both methods simultaneously from the same application or application family.

Example 3.1: Using gettext()

```
#include <stdio.h>
#include <locale.h>
#include <libintl.h>

int
main(int argc, char *argv[])
{
  printf("LANG=%s\n", getenv("LANG"));

  /* initialize LC_MESSAGES according to
   * LC_ALL, LC_MESSAGES, or LANG
   */

  setlocale(LC_ALL, "");

  printf ("dirname=%s\n",
    bindtextdomain("ghw", "/usr/share/locale/"));

  printf("domainname=%s\n", textdomain("ghw"));

  /* Look up MSGID in the current default message catalog for the
   * current LC_MESSAGES locale.  If not found, gettext() returns
   * MSGID itself (the default text).
   */

  printf(gettext("Hello World\n"));

  printf(gettext("The value of Open Standards \
  is only evident to Open Minds\n"));

  printf(gettext("Good Bye\n"));

  exit(0);
}
```

3.3   PAM

The are many different ways an application can authenticate a user with the system. Applications that use hardcoded calls to getpwnam(3) or shadow(3) are limited in that they can only work on a system configured accordingly. The Pluggable Authentication Module (PAM) abstracts the mechanics of authentication from the application and enables the local system administrator to choose how individual applications will authenticate users. Example 3.2 shows an application using pam_authenticate(3).

Example 3.2: Using pam_authenticate(3)

```
#include <security/pam_appl.h>
#include <security/pam_misc.h>
#include <stdio.h>

static struct pam_conv conv = {
      misc_conv,
          NULL
};

int main(int argc, char *argv[])
{
  pam_handle_t *pamh;
  int pam_status;
  char *user;

  pam_status = pam_start("lsb_login", NULL, &conv, &pamh);

  if (pam_status == PAM_SUCCESS)
     pam_status = pam_authenticate(pamh, 0);

  if (pam_status == PAM_SUCCESS) {
     pam_get_item(pamh, PAM_USER, (const void **)&user);
     fprintf(stdout, "Greetings %s\n", user);
  } else {
     printf("%s\n", pam_strerror(pamh, pam_status));
  }

  pam_end(pamh, pam_status);
}
```

The pam_start(3) call registers the application with the specified service. After the user is vouched for by pam_authenticate(3), the application can safely trust the user's identity and privileges.

3.4   JAVA

Those wanting to develop Java applications that are compatible across different JVMs should follow the Java API Specification.[1] Java is not native to Linux nor UNIX, so it is out of scope of the LSB.

Applications that use the Java Native Interface (JNI)[2] do have native Linux object code that can and should be LSB-conformant. JNI object code can be LSB-certified.

3.5   kill(3)

Passing process ID -1 to kill(3) doesn't affect the calling process. This was a deliberate decision after the unpopular experiment of including the calling process in the 2.5.1 kernel.[3]

3.6   ioctl(3)

The LSB has its own definition of ioctl(3) and does not reference ISO/IEC 9945.

---

1. http://java.sun.com/reference/api/index.html

2. http://java.sun.com/docs/books/tutorial/native1.1/concepts/index.html

3. *What does it mean to signal everybody?*, Linux Weekly News, 20 December 2001 (http://lwn.net/2001/1220/kernel.php3).

3.7   IP INFORMATION

With the advent of IPv6, `gethostbyname(3)` has been replaced with routines
such as `getaddrinfo(3)` and `getnameinfo(3)`. For better compatibility,
these newer IPv6 functions should be used (Example 3.3).

Example 3.3: Using IPv6 Functions

```
#include <netdb.h>
#include <stdio.h>

int main(int argc, char **argv) {

struct addrinfo *res, *r;
struct addrinfo hints;
struct sockaddr *sa;
int rc;
char * proto;

char hostbuf[NI_MAXHOST];
char servbuf[NI_MAXSERV];

  bzero(&hints,sizeof(hints));
  hints.ai_family = PF_UNSPEC;
  hints.ai_socktype = SOCK_STREAM;
  hints.ai_flags = AI_CANONNAME;

  if ((rc = getaddrinfo("linuxbase.org", NULL, &hints, &res))) {
    fprintf(stderr, "%s\n", gai_strerror(rc));
    exit(2);
  }

  for (r = res; r; r = r->ai_next) {

    if(r->ai_family == AF_INET6){
        inet_ntop(AF_INET6,
        &(((struct sockaddr_in6 *)r->ai_addr)->sin6_addr),
        hostbuf, sizeof(hostbuf));
        proto = "IPv6";
    } else if (r->ai_family == AF_INET) {
```

```
        inet_ntop(AF_INET,
        &(((struct sockaddr_in *)r->ai_addr)->sin_addr),
        hostbuf, sizeof(hostbuf));
        proto = "IPv4";
    }

    printf("getaddrinfo(3): %s address = %s\n", proto, hostbuf);

    bzero(hostbuf, sizeof(hostbuf)); /* clear */

    if (getnameinfo(r->ai_addr, r->ai_addrlen,
        hostbuf, sizeof(hostbuf),
        servbuf, sizeof(servbuf),
        NI_NAMEREQD|NI_NUMERICSERV)){
        printf("getnameinfo(3): could not find IP.\n");
    } else {
        printf("getnameinfo(3): host = %s\n", hostbuf);
    }
  }
  freeaddrinfo(res);
}
```

3.8 O_LARGEFILE

When available, the LSB permits Linux implementations to set O_LARGEFILE
with fcntl(3). Applications should set this flag explicitly when needed, and
not expect the runtime to set it by default (Example 3.4).

Example 3.4: O_LARGEFILE **with** fcntl(3) **Function**

```
#ifdef __USE_LARGEFILE64
  int oflag = fcntl(fd, F_GETFL, 0);
  if (oflag & O_LARGEFILE) {
    debug("O_LARGEFILE was implicitly set");  // BAD
  }
  oflag |= O_LARGEFILE;            // GOOD
  fcntl(fd, F_SETFL, oflag);
#endif
```

3.9   EISDIR(3)

If the path argument of unlink(3) specifies a directory, the implementation may return EISDIR instead of EPERM as specified by the Single UNIX Specification (Example 3.5).

Example 3.5: EISDIR

```
#include <sys/stat.h>
#include <sys/types.h>
#include <fcntl.h>
#include <errno.h>
#include <stdio.h>

main() {

  char *newdir = "/tmp/example_dir";

  if (0 != mkdir(newdir, O_CREAT)) {
    printf("mkdir %s: %s\n", newdir, strerror(errno));
  }

  if (0 != unlink(newdir)) {

    switch (errno) {
    case EISDIR:
      printf("EISDIR: %s is a directory\n", newdir);
      break;
    case EPERM:
      printf("EPERM: operation not permitted for %s\n", newdir);
      break;
    default:
      perror ("unlink");
      break;
    }
  }
}
```

3.10 `waitpid(3)`

The LSB has deprecated the use of `waitid(3)`. Applications should call the `waitpid(3)` interface as specified in the Single UNIX Specification, but implementations need not support the X/Open System Interfaces Extension (XSI) functionality of `WCONTINUED` or `WIFCONTINUED` (Example 3.6).

3.11 PARSING OF COMMAND OPTIONS

The GNU `getopt(3)` function parses command-line arguments as specified by the Single UNIX Specification Version 3, when the plus sign "+" is the first character in the operation string of the function's third parameter.

The GNU operation string flags "`W;`" (to enable long options), "`-`" (to return '`\1`' for invalid options), and "`::`" (to enable optional flag arguments) should not be used when trying to maintain SUSv3 compliance (Example 3.7).

3.12 LSB Don'ts

This chapter is about portability etiquette. As an open systems developer, there are things you should not do. You should realize that the compromises to ensure portability outweight the short-term benefits of tuning to a specific release.

3.12.1 `/proc`

The LSB only specifies the `/proc/cpuinfo` file and its keys. Applications should not attempt to collect any other data from the `/proc` filesystem, because it is unspecified and unreliable.

Example 3.6: Using `waitpid(3)`

```c
#include <assert.h>
#include <errno.h>
#include <stdio.h>
#include <stdlib.h>

int main (void)
{
  int rc, status;
  pid_t pid;

  pid = fork();

  if (pid < 0) {
    perror("fork");
    exit(1);
  }

  if (0 == pid) {
    printf("\tChild process (pid=%d) running\n",getpid());
    sleep (10);
    printf("\tChild process (pid=%d) terminating\n",getpid());
    exit(0);
  }

  printf("Parent process (pid=%d) waiting for child (pid=%d)\n",
    getpid(), pid);

  rc=waitpid(pid, &status, 0);

  printf("Parent process (pid=%d) continuing ", getpid());
  printf("after the termination of child (pid=%d).\n", pid);
  printf("Status=%08X Return Code=%d\n", status, rc);

  if (rc < 0) {
    perror ("waitpid");
    exit(2);
  }

  exit(0);
}
```

Example 3.7: Command Options

```
#include <unistd.h>
#include <stdio.h>

int
main (int argc, char **argv)
{
  int aflag = 0;
  int bflag = 0;
  char *cvalue = NULL;
  int errflg = 0;
  int index, c;

  /* the plus sign is required to permanently set
   * POSIXLY_CORRECT
   */

  while ((c = getopt (argc, argv, "+abc:")) != -1)
    switch (c) {
    case 'a':
      aflag = 1;
      break;
    case 'b':
      bflag - 1;
      break;
    case 'c':
      cvalue = optarg;
      break;
    case ':':
      fprintf (stderr,
        "Option -%c requires an operand\n",
        optopt);

      errflg++;
      return 1;
    case '?':
      fprintf (stderr, "Unknown option -%c\n", optopt);
      errflg++;
      return 1;
    default:
      fprintf (stderr, "Hopelessly lost\n");
      errflg++;
      break;
    }
```

```
if (errflg) {
  fprintf (stderr, "USAGE: %s -a -b -c file", argv[0]);
  exit(1);
}

printf ("aflag = %d, bflag = %d, cvalue = %s\n",
  aflag, bflag, cvalue);

for (index = optind; index < argc; index++)
  printf ("Operand argument %s\n", argv[index]);

exit(0);
}
```

3.12.2   Berkeley Database

The Berkeley Database (DB)[4] is a popular data management engine used by many Linux applications; however, at the time of publication of this book, DB does not meet the LSB Futures selection criteria.[5]

3.12.3   Kernel

The Application Programming Interfaces (APIs) provided by the system libraries abstract the operating system resource management of the kernel. It is improper for a portable application to use the private interfaces of a system, so you should take care to only code with the interfaces defined by the LSB Written Specification.

3.12.4   Drivers

On UNIX and GNU/Linux systems, "a file is a file," and a device is just another file that can be opened, read from, written to, and closed. An application should not try to mimic the functionality of a driver; it must simply interact with the device in the protocol of the driver.

---

4. Sleepycat Software, makers of Berkeley DB (http://www.sleepycat.com/).

5. http://www.linuxbase.org/futures/criteria/

3.12.5 Desktop

When developing an application that uses a Graphical User Interface (GUI), it is best to concentrate on perfecting its usability and portability rather than desktop integration. No one can guarantee a specific window manager or desktop that the end user will be using, so it is best to not limit the application by loading it down with desktop-specific features.

3.12.6 Threads

At the time of the writing of this book, the current Linux distributions were in various states of supporting Linux theads, Next Generation POSIX Threads (NGPT), and Native POSIX Threads Library (NPTL). The next generation of Linux distributions will be supporting NPTL. LSB v2.0 specifies pThreads as implemented by NPTL and the 2.6 Linux kernel. Applications and middleware should migrate to NPTL.

3.12.7 gets(3)

Although `gets(3)` is specified by POSIX, the LSB has deprecated it. Both the LSB and POSIX recommend the use of `fgets(3)` instead of `gets(3)`.

3.12.8 system(3)

The LSB has its own definition of `system(3)` which does not reference ISO/IEC 9945. Although it is specified, for portability it is recommended instead to use `popen(3)`, `execl(3)`, `execle(3)`, or `execv(3)`.

3.12.9 ncurses

Both the LSB and the SUS specify the use of `curses.h`. For source code portability, do not use `ncurses.h`.

3.12.10 malloc(3)

When using `malloc(3)`, include `stdlib.h` instead of `malloc.h` because, along with compiler option `-lmalloc`, these are later used for debugging (Example 3.8).

Example 3.8: `malloc(3)`

```
#ifdef DEBUG
#include <malloc.h>
#endif
#include <stdlib.h>
```

## CHAPTER FOUR

Packaging
Your LSB Application

The LSB specifies application packaging in order to ensure compatibility between applications and Linux distributions. Packaging can be distribution-specific, so it is possible that your application will not run across distributions if you do not follow the LSB packaging specifications. In this chapter you will learn about the RPM file format and the correct locations for installing your applications.

4.1 USING RPM FOR PACKAGING

There are over one hundred Linux distributions for end users to run their applications on.[1] To ensure that applications will be able to install successfully, the LSB specifies the RPM file format as the best possible solution. It is the responsibility of an LSB Certified Runtime Environment (that is, an operating system or Linux distribution) to be able to install RPM packaged applications. The book *Maximum RPM* by Edward Bailey and the RPM Web site[2] are excellent resources for learning to create RPM packages. For the examples in this chapter, don't worry about the details, but pay attention to the guidelines on where to install everything.

For reliability, an application cannot be dependent on itself for installation because ad hoc installers are not guaranteed to work. The RPM file format has

---

1. DistroWatch (`http://www.distrowatch.org/`).

2. `http://www.rpm.org/`

been specified because it is accepted by many Linux distributions; however, you may use another packaging format if the install program your application is dependent on is LSB-certified and known to be previously installed.[3]

4.1.1   RPM Checking

The LSB package check command, **lsbpkgchk**, is a program that verifies that a package and its contents conform to the LSB Written Specification. The version number it displays refers to the version of the specification that it was built for, not the version of the command itself.

4.2   INSTALLING YOUR APPLICATION IN THE RIGHT PLACE

Software developers and independent software vendors (ISVs) have differing ideas about the best place to install applications and software packages. Some install in `/usr/bin/` or `/usr/local/bin/`, others prefer the `/opt/` directory. Your preferences might vary depending on whether you come from a UNIX System V, Berkeley Software Distribution (BSD), or GNU/Linux background. These unpredictable variations cause file and directory naming conflicts that sometimes disrupt software installation, removal, and upgrades.

The Filesystem Hierarchy Standard (FHS),[4] referenced by the LSB, provides guidelines and defines requirements for file and directory placement. The FHS promotes the interoperability of applications, system administration tools, development tools, and scripts. The FHS explains in detail the content and purpose of each of the primary directories. Figure 4.1 shows the directory structure as specified by the FHS.

In addition to the FHS, the System V Application Binary Interface,[5] the Intel Binary Compatibility Standard V.2 (iBCS2), the Common Operating System Environment (COSE), the Linux Standard Base (LSB), and the UNIX

---

3. Portions of this chapter were derived with permission from "Where to Install My Products on Linux?" by George Kraft IV, *Linux Journal*, November 2000.

4. `http://www.pathname.com/fhs/`

5. System V Application Binary Interface, Dec. 17, 2003, The SCO Group (`http://www.caldera.com/developers/gabi/2003-12-17/contents.html`).

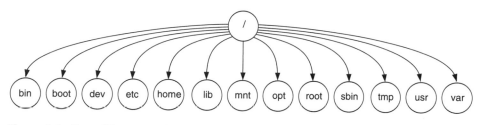

Figure 4.1: Base Filesytem Hierarchy Specified by the FHS

community in general have already established the `/opt/` directory for add-on software. The following list is a compilation of best practices for installing applications.

 In the following list, `package` is the product name of an application and `provider` is a LANANA-registered vendor name.

- The applications of the base operating system, or "the Linux distribution," are the only ones allowed to be installed in the `/sbin/`, `/bin/`, and `/usr/` directories.

- System administrators who build packages from source—either source packages (`srpm`) or tape-archives (`tar`)—should install in the `/usr/local/bin/` directory, and must avoid the temptation to install in the system directories.

- Add-on binary-only packaged applications must be installed in the `/opt/package/` or `/opt/provider/` directory. For example, the binary executables should reside in their respective `/opt/provider/bin/` directories.

- Manual pages for applications must be located in their respective `/opt/package/share/man/` or `/opt/provider/share/man/` directories. Documentation other than man pages should be located in the corresponding `/opt/package/share/doc/` or `/opt/provider/share/doc/` directories.

- Host-specific configuration files for `/opt/` binary executables should go in the `/etc/opt/package/` or `/etc/opt/provider/` directory (all host-specific system configuration files reside in these directories).

- Variable files in a package, or files that change during the normal course of system runtime, go in the `/var/opt/package/` and `/var/opt/provider/` directories.

Exceptions can be made to these rules if it is necessary for a package to install or create files elsewhere. For example, if a package creates a new device, it installs in the `/dev/` directory.

The system administrator should create a separate disk partition for the `/opt/` filesystem, and end users should add `/opt/package/bin/` and `/opt/bin/` to their PATH environment variables. Usually the end user's shell will find applications in their respective `/opt/package/bin/` directories; however, the system administrator may have created symbolic links or wrapper scripts in `/opt/` for each package using **setup-opt.sh**.

```
# setup-opt.sh /opt/whizbang/bin/widgets
# setup-opt.sh /opt/whizbang/man/man1/widgets.1
```

4.3   PACKAGE NAMING

To avoid conflicts between native distribution packages and LSB-conformant packages, a naming scheme was specified. Names of all LSB-compliant packages begin with `lsb-`. If the name of the package contains only one hyphen, then the name must be assigned by the Linux Assigned Names and Numbers Authority.[6] If the name of the package contains more than one hyphen, then the portion of the package name between the first and second hyphens must be either an LSB provider name assigned by the LANANA, or one of the owner's fully-qualified domain names in lowercase.

4.3.1   Init Script Naming

The LANANA init script names are used by LSB-compliant applications and distributions when naming init scripts placed in the `/etc/init.d` directory. Alternatively, it is also possible to use a script name that begins with your fully qualified Internet domain name or your LSB provider name.

---

6. `http://www.lanana.org/`

Since all init scripts live in the same directory, a similar scheme has been specified to avoid clashes between init scripts for packages. The LSB Written Specification states that init scripts can be in one of three namespaces:

1. **Assigned namespace** This namespace consists of names that only use the character set `[a-z0-9]`. These names must be reserved through LANANA.

2. **Hierarchical namespace** This namespace consists of script names that look like this: `[hier1]-[hier2]-...-[name]`, where *name* uses the character set `[a-z0-9]` and there may be one or more `[hiern]` components. The `[hier1]` may either be an LSB provider name assigned by the LANANA, or it may be the owner's DNS name in lowercase, with at least one period character (".").

3. **Reserved namespace** This namespace consists of script names that begin with the underscore character ("_"), and it is reserved for distribution use only. This namespace should be used for core packages only, and in general, use of this namespace is highly discouraged.

4.3.2   Cron Script Naming

The LANANA Cron Script registry defines a reserved list of script names to be used in the `/etc/cron.d` directory in an LSB Runtime Environment. Alternatively, it is also possible to use a script name that begins with your fully qualified Internet domain name or your LSB provider name.

4.4   EXAMPLE: PACKAGING AND INSTALLING AN APPLICATION

Example 4.1 shows how to package and install a fictional software suite called Widgets according to LSB packaging specifications. The `widgets-1.2-3.spec` RPM configuration file is used to package the software for the `/opt/` directory. The `%files` directive (line 17) is followed by a list of pathnames which should be packaged. The `Prefix` tag (line 8) is how the package is made relocatable. The value of the tag defines the part of the path that can be varied at installation time.

Example 4.1: RPM Spec File for Widgets

```
   #
   # RPM Package Manager (RPM) spec file for Widgets :-)
   #
   Summary: Some generic program
 5 Name: widgets
   Version: 1.2
   Release: 3
   Prefix: /opt
   Copyright: Commercial
10 Group: Application/Productivity
   URL: http://www.whizbangwidgets.com/
   Vendor: WhizBang Widgets
   Packager: John Doe <jd@whizbangwidgets.com>
   %description
15 This is a demonstration of a relocatable RPM package for a
   fictional productivity application.
   %files
   /opt/whizbang/bin/widgets
   /opt/whizbang/man/widgets.1
20 /etc/opt/whizbang/widgets.conf
   # Post-install stuff would go here.
   #EOF
```

1. Build the RPM package for Widgets (`widgets-1.2-3.i486`), as shown in Example 4.2, using `widgets-1.2-3.spec` as the input file. You can use **rpm** to build and produce a source package file (`widgets-1.2-3.src.rpm`) and a binary package file (`widgets-1.2-3.i486.rpm`) from this input.

Example 4.2: Building an RPM Package for Widgets

```
# rpm -ba /usr/src/redhat/SPECS/widgets-1.2-3.spec
Processing files: widgets
Finding provides...
Finding requires...
Prereqs: /bin/sh
Wrote: /usr/src/redhat/SRPMS/widgets-1.2-3.src.rpm
Wrote: /usr/src/redhat/RPMS/i486/widgets-1.2-3.i486.rpm
```

2. Install Widgets on the system from the binary package (`widgets-1.2-3.i486.rpm`), as shown in Example 4.3.

Example 4.3: Installing an RPM Package for Widgets

```
# rpm -i /usr/src/redhat/RPMS/i486/widgets-1.2-3.i486.rpm
```

Widgets is now installed in `/opt/whizbang/bin/`.

3. Run Widgets from the command line, as shown in Example 4.4.

Example 4.4: Running Widgets

```
$ /opt/whizbang/bin/widgets
```

---

4. As the system administrator, create a symbolic link to `/opt/whizbang/bin/widgets` from `/opt/bin/widgets`, and to `/opt/whizbang/lib/libwidget.so` from `/opt/lib/libwidget.so` (Example 4.5). Per the FHS, this cannot be done at the post-install stage automatically because the package does not own the `/opt/bin/` directory domain. Only the system administrator has the authority to make a global configuration that may impact other applications.

Example 4.5: Manually Creating Symbolic Links for Widgets

```
# ln -s /opt/whizbang/bin/widgets /opt/bin/widgets
# ln -s /opt/whizbang/lib/libwidget.so /opt/lib/libwidget.so
```

As illustrated in Figure 4.2, the symbolic link will make it easier for the end user to run Widgets.

5. Uninstall the `widgets-1.2-3` RPM package, and reinstall it in an alternate location in the `/usr/local` directory, as shown in Example 4.6.

The system administrator should not forget to fix any manual symbolic links that may have been made in `/opt/bin/`.

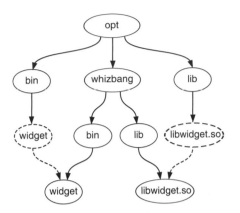

Figure 4.2: Simple Packaging

Example 4.6: Relocating Widgets

```
# rpm -e widgets-1.2-3
# cd /usr/src/redhat/RPMS/i486/
# rpm -i --prefix /usr/local widgets-1.2-3.i486.rpm
```

4.5   ADVANCED PACKAGING

It has been demonstrated that add-on binary-only applications are to be installed in the /opt/*package*/bin/ and /opt/*provider*/bin/ directories. The basics of creating a flexible relocatable RPM package have been demonstrated by being able to override the default /opt/ destination and select an alternate location. Now let's look at more advanced scenarios involving packaging multiple products, packaging for multiple architectures, packaging for multiple versions of a product, or any combinations thereof.

4.5.1   Packaging Multiple Products

Recall the WhizBang Widgets example in this chapter. What if you want to ship another product called Gadgets? To support multiple products by one vendor, they should all be based off of the /opt/*provider*/*package*/ directory as illustrated in Figure 4.3. Since the LANANA-registered WhizBang owns

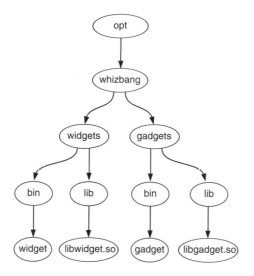

Figure 4.3: Packaging Multiple Products

the `/opt/whizbang/` directory, the two most common ways that directory can be used are either to share the `bin` and `lib` subdirectories or to keep them separate in their own `/opt/whizbang/widgets/` and `/opt/whizbang/gadgets/` subdirectories. If they are kept separate, then symbolic links or wrapper scripts in `/opt/whizbang/bin/` can be redirected to `/opt/whizbang/widgets/bin/` and `/opt/whizbang/gadgets/bin/`. In either case, `/opt/whizbang/bin/` should be added to the end user's `PATH` environment variable.

4.5.2   Packaging for Multiple Architectures

To simultaneously support both 32-bit and 64-bit PowerPC versions of Wid-gets on a PPC64 system, they need to be separated into their own respective architecture subdirectories such as `/opt/whizbang/widgets/ppc32/` and `/opt/whizbang/widgets/ppc64/` as illustrated in Figure 4.4. The system administrator could set up a default PPC32 or PPC64 behavior by creating a symbolic link from `/opt/whizbang/widgets/ppc32/bin/` back to `/opt/whizbang/widgets/bin/`, or `/opt/whizbang/widgets/ppc32/lib/` back to `/opt/whizbang/widgets/lib/`. In either case,

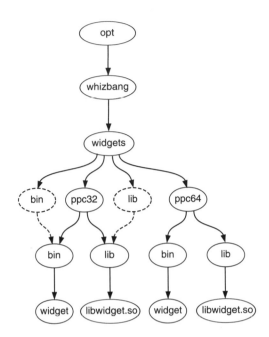

Figure 4.4: Packaging for Multiple Architectures

`/opt/whizbang/widgets/bin/` should be added to the end user's PATH environment variable.

4.5.3   Packaging Multiple Product Versions

To simultaneously support multiple versions of same products, they need to be separated into their own respective version subdirectories, such as `/opt/whizbang/widgets/v1/` and `/opt/whizbang/widgets/v2/` as illustrated in Figure 4.5. The system administrator could set up a default v1 or v2 behavior by creating a symbolic link from `/opt/whizbang/widgets/v1/bin/` back to `/opt/whizbang/widgets/bin/` or `/opt/whizbang/widgets/v2/lib/` back to `/opt/whizbang/widgets/lib/` (Example 4.7). In either case, `/opt/whizbang/widgets/bin/` should be added to the end user's PATH environment variable.

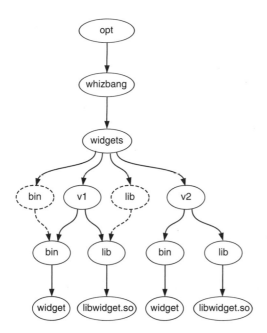

Figure 4.5: Packaging Multiple Product Versions

Example 4.7: Symbolic Link Widgets during Post Install

```
%post
P=$RPM_INSTALL_PREFIX/whizbang/widgets
mkdir $P/bin > /dev/null 2>&1
ln -fs $P/ppc32/bin/widgets $P/bin/widgets
# EOF
```

4.5.4 Packaging Multiple Versions of Multiple Products for Multiple Architectures

To simultaneously support multiple versions of multiple products on multiple architectures, they need to be separated into their own respective subdirectories, such as /opt/whizbang/widgets/v1/ppc32/ or /opt/whizbang/gadgets/v2/ppc64/ as illustrated in Figure 4.6. The

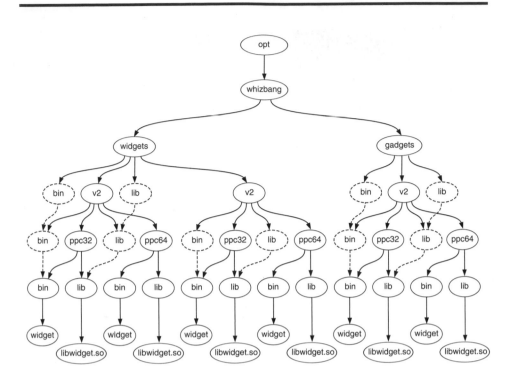

Figure 4.6: Packaging Multiple Versions of Multiple Products for Multiple Architectures

system administrator could set up a default v1 or v2 and/or PPC32 or PPC64 behavior by creating a symbolic link from `/opt/whizbang/widgets/v1/ppc32/bin/` to `/opt/whizbang/widgets/bin/`. In either case, `/opt/whizbang/widgets/bin/` should be added to the end user's `PATH` environment variable.

CHAPTER FIVE

Migrating
Solaris Applications to Linux

One of the consequences of the increasing popularity of Linux is that companies are enthusiastic to migrate their existing applications and development environments to Linux. An application following the standards will be easier to port than a nonconformant application. Since Linux and Solaris share the common API sets of UNIX, migrating from Solaris to Linux is easier than from an operating system with different APIs, such as Microsoft Windows.

This chapter provides an outline of the advantages of such a migration and the path that can be taken. In addition to providing the toolsets that can be used in the process of migration, some standard-related porting issues are also discussed.

5.1   ROADMAP TO PORT

Developing a portable application is not a easy task. Even though both Solaris and Linux are UNIX variants, there are lots of differences in the APIs, system calls, and other components. Any Linux distribution comes with ample documentation on how to make use of these interfaces to develop applications. However, the documentation is not always clear, and standards are very versatile. One related standard is the Portable Operating System Interface (POSIX) specification (see Section 2.2.1). If you develop your application to be in compliance with this specification, it is much easier to port.

Developing an application for a platform also requires a rich set of tools. Linux as a platform is bundled with many such tools that are open source in nature. These tools include code editors, code formating tools, compilers, linkers, and debuggers. Also available from various vendors are the commercial equivalent of these tools.

The steps outlined here are just one way of performing a seamless migration; there are many other ways. Selection of a migration path depends on the amount of resources and time that can be spent on this task. Once a path is chosen, it has to be carried out with proper planning and small step executions.

The idea of this roadmap is to adapt the Solaris application to be migrated so that it can run on a SPARC version of Linux. Once this is done, then the application migration to the target Linux platform can be carried out with relatively little effort.

5.1.1   Step 1: Obtain the Necessary Linux Distributions

In order to carry out this migration scheme, it is necessary to use two different Linux distributions: one Linux distribution for SPARC and another Linux distribution specific to the target platform.

Linux/SPARC, available since 1994, is as old and mature as a regular Linux. Major Linux vendors, such as Red Hat and SuSE, have also released their versions of Linux/SPARC. Linux/SPARC is available for almost the entire line of SPARC hardware, including versions for 32-bit and 64-bit processors.

Linux is also available for different hardware platforms such as Intel compatible PCs, PPC (PowerPC), Alpha processors, Itanium, and mainframes. The list of available vendors for various platforms is available on the Web.[1] This list includes both commercial and free versions of Linux. You can use this list to determine the Linux version based on the target platform, its bundled features and necessary funds.

5.1.2   Step 2: Download the Necessary GNU Tools

GNU has the tools needed for developmental work called GCC (GNU Compiler Collection). GCC supports various languages such as C, C++, Fortran,

---

1. Linux Distributions (`http://www.linux.org/dist/`).

and even Java. A complete list of GNU tools is available online.[2] GNU tools favor developing a portable source code while reducing the time spent in the migration process. Even a Solaris developer with little Linux knowledge can start producing code for the target Linux platform with these tools.

GNU tools necessary for the Solaris environment can be downloaded from `http://www.sunfreeware.com/`. Most GNU tools for Solaris are available free of cost from this site. GNU tools for Linux on SPARC as well as the target platform are also shipped with their respective distributions.

5.1.3   Step 3: Build the C/C++ Applications on Solaris

Once all the build tools are procured, start the build process on Solaris. Use the GNU **gmake** utility instead of **make** to build the source code. There are considerable differences between these utilities even though they both serve the same purpose. The makefile created for the Solaris **make** utility when used with the **gmake** utility might generate errors depending on the constructs used in it. The respective **gmake**[3] and **make**[4] tool documentation is the best source for resolving these errors.

In spite of the differences between these tools, they also share some common rules and suffixes. The targets, macros, and variables shown in Table 5.1 can be used interchangeably as they have the same meaning in both utilities.

After modifying the makefile to comply with **gmake** rules, the next step is to try the GNU compilers instead of their Solaris counterparts. The **gcc** compiler should be used instead of **cc** and **g++** instead of **C++**. Once the GNU compiler is used, there will be lot of errors that can be categorized into errors due to command-line option differences and errors due to coding differences. However, both these kinds of errors can be resolved mostly by referring to the compiler documentation:

 • Using and Porting the GNU Compiler Collection (GCC)[5]

---

2. `http://www.gnu.org/directory/GNU/`

3. GNU **make** (`http://www.gnu.org/software/make/manual/make.html`).

4. *Managing Projects with make* (`http://www.oreilly.com/catalog/make2/`).

5. `http://gcc.gnu.org/onlinedocs/gcc-2.95.2/gcc_toc.html`

Table 5.1: Common Targets, Macros, and Variables in **make** and GNU **gmake**

Targets	`.DEFAULT, .IGNORE, .PRECIOUS, .SILENT, .SUFFIX`
Internal macros	`$*, $%, $?, $<, $@, $$@, $(F), $(D)`
Predefined macros	`ar, as, cc, ld, lex, lint, m2c, pc, rm -f, yacc`
Environment variable	`MAKEFLAGS`
Variables	`CC, CFLAGS, CPPFLAGS, FC, FFLAGS, LEX, LFLAGS, YACC, YFLAGS, LD, LDFLAGS`

- C User's Guide[6]
- C++ User's Guide[7]

Once the application gets compiled for the Solaris environment, the process has to be repeated on a Linux version running on the SPARC hardware. Since the application is already compliant with the GNU tools, the only problems that might arise will be due to the runtime application programming interfaces. These APIs differences need to be corrected for a fully compliant application. The following are some major differences between Linux and Solaris.

System calls   There are name differences between Solaris and Linux APIs that provide support for logical volume support, file access control list, and system audit log. STREAMS support, which is useful for writing stream-based network device drivers, is not available on Linux but is available on Solaris. So the solution for a problem like this is to get a third-party, independently developed solution or rewrite the application to use a related technology. In this case, POSIX sockets can be used instead of STREAMS for networking.

Library differences   The standard C++ libraries that are available on Linux include support for most of the functionalities. Solaris has some

---

6. `http://docs.sun.com/db/doc/817-5064/`

7. `http://docs.sun.com/db/doc/817-5070/`

additional libraries such as compat=4, classic iostreams, and math library with support for ASCII-encoded decimal conversions. If the application to be ported uses any of these additional libraries, it has to be modified to use the standard C++ libraries.

Threading differences   Solaris processes are based on threads called *lightweight processes* (LWP). In current Linux implementation, threads are based on processes. There are two types of threads available in Solaris, POSIX threads and native threading model. Linux supports POSIX threads, so all applications that use native threads should be modified to use POSIX threads.

5.1.4   Step 4: Build the Application on Linux for the Target Platform

Install Linux on the target platform and rebuild the modified application from previous step.

5.2   ISSUES WITH PORTING

Porting applications from a Solaris platform to Linux platform may be considered an easy task because of the application level portability provided by the GNU C libraries of the Linux platform. In most cases, the application can be ported by simply recompiling the program. But if the code has any system or hardware-dependent constructs, then some modification is needed to carry out a complete porting. The complexity of such a porting effort is directly proportional to the amount of system and hardware-dependent code. If the application uses only standard language constructs and does not take platform considerations, then such an application will be less complicated to port. If the application uses non-POSIX constructs or platform-specific optimizations, then the porting will be harder. Typically, a Java application would fall in the first category, and a non-POSIX C program would fall in the second category. Some of the issues related to porting are explained in the following sections.

5.2.1   Byte Ordering

Byte ordering, or *endianness*, is the property of a data element that refers to how its bytes are stored or addressed in memory. This property is determined by the CPU architecture of the platform. There are two possible values of endianness, *big endian* and *little endian*.

5.2.1.1   Big Endian

In this type of byte ordering the most significant byte is stored at the lowest storage address—for example, the most significant byte is stored in the left-most position. Sun SPARC, HP Precision, and the IBM PPC use this type of ordering (Example 5.1).

Example 5.1: Big Endian Ordering

Data: 0x33445566
Storage:

Byte 0	Byte 1	Byte 2	Byte 3
33 (most significant)	44	55	66

5.2.1.2   Little Endian

In this type of byte ordering the least significant byte is stored at the lowest storage address—for example, the least significant byte is stored in the leftmost position. Intel and DEC architectures use this ordering (Example 5.2).

Example 5.2: Little Endian Ordering

Data: 0x33445566
Storage:

Byte 0	Byte 1	Byte 2	Byte 3
66 (least significant)	55	44	33

5.2.1.3   Byte Ordering and Union Data Structure

The byte ordering discussed in the previous sections will become an issue in porting if the code uses the union data structure. Union is a data structure to manipulate different types of data in the same storage area. It is completely the compiler's responsibility to manage the size and alignment of the data stored in that storage area. For example, consider the union shown in Example 5.3.

Example 5.3: Union Data Structure

```
union char_int {
  char a[4];
  int i;
}char_int;
```

Consider the code in Example 5.4 that uses the above union.

Example 5.4: Wrong Use of a Union

```
// define an instance variable of the union
union char_int cint;
// define a variable to hold the computation result
int result;
// assign a value to the union using the integer variable
cint.i = 0x10394500;
// divide the constant 100 with the union's MSB,
// that is, its first byte
result = 100/a[0];
```

This example uses the knowledge of byte ordering to retrieve the most significant byte of the integer data. While this code will work properly on big-endian architecture, when it is ported to a little-endian machine, the code will fail because of a divide by zero error. To make it portable either the byte ordering information should not be used inside the code, or the byte information has to be defined conditionally by compilation parameters (Example 5.5).

Byte ordering may also cause problems for network data transfer. Most of the modern network protocols take the endianness into account. These protocols use the External Data Representation (XDR) ordering to transfer data. Data from different source environments is converted to this representation before starting a transfer. Data will convert back to the native representation of the target environment at the finish of transfer. Distributed applications that do raw data transfers should also account for the endianness.

Example 5.5: Correct Use of a Union

```
// Portability code added
#ifdef BIGENDIAN
const int MSBBYTE=0;
#else
const int MSBBYTE=3;
#endif

// define an instance variable of the union
union char_int cint;
// define a variable to hold the computation result
int result;
// assign a value to the union using the integer variable
cint.i = 0x10394500;
// divide the constant 100 with the union's MSB,
// that is, its first byte
result = 100/a[MSBBYTE];
```

The standard C library provides many routines to do this conversion. APIs, such as the following one, provide a way to ensure platform independence while doing the network transfer.

- `ntohl()` converts `unsigned int` from XDR to native.

- `ntohs()` converts `unsigned short` from XDR to native.

- `htonl()` converts `unsigned int` from native to XDR.

- `htons()` converts `unsigned short` from native to XDR.

5.3   SIGNAL HANDLING

Signals are the means to notify a process or thread of the occurrence of an event. In this area, Linux supports most of the signals supported by UNIX systems such as SVR4 and the BSD implementations. However, there are some exceptions that need to be considered.

- `SIGEMT`, representing hardware fault, is not supported.
- `SIGINFO`, representing keyboard information requests, is supported.
- `SIGSYS`, representing invalid system call, is not supported.
- `SIGABRT` and `SIGIOT` are identical.
- `SIGIO`, `SIGPOLL`, and `SIGURG` are identical.
- `SIGBUS` is defined as `SIGUNUSED` because there is no "bus error" in Linux.

Table 5.2 lists various signals and their meaning in Solaris and Linux environments. This table can be used to verify if the signals used in your code have different semantics in Linux.

Table 5.2: Semantics of Signals in Solaris and Linux

Signal	*Solaris*	*Linux*
SIGHUP	Terminate	Ignore
SIGINT	Terminate	Ignore
SIGQUIT	Terminate, core	Terminate, core
SIGILL	Terminate, core	Terminate, core
SIGTRAP	Terminate, core	Ignore
SIGABRT	Terminate, core	Terminate, core
SIGEMT	Terminate, core	Not supported on Linux
SIGFPE	Terminate, core	Terminate, core
SIGKILL	Terminate	Terminate
SIGBUS	Terminate, core	Terminate, core
SIGSEGV	Terminate, core	Terminate, core
SIGSYS	Terminate, core	Not supported on Linux
SIGPIPE	Terminate	Ignore

Table 5.2 *(Continued)*

Signal	Solaris	Linux
SIGALRM	Terminate	Ignore
SIGTERM	Terminate	Terminate
SIGUSR1	Terminate	Ignore
SIGUSR2	Terminate	Ignore
SIGCHLD	Ignore	Ignore
SIGPWR	Ignore	Ignore
SIGWINCH	Ignore	Process stop
SIGURG	Ignore	Ignore
SIGPOLL	Terminate	Not supported on Linux
SIGSTOP	Process stop	Process stop
SIGSTP	Process stop	Process stop
SIGCONT	Ignore	Ignore
SIGTTIN	Process stop	Process stop
SIGTTOU	Process stop	Process stop
SIGVTALRM	Terminate	Terminate, core
SIGPROF	Terminate	Ignore
SIGXCPU	Terminate, core	Terminate, core
SIGXFSZ	Terminate, core	Terminate, core
SIGWAITING	Ignore	Not supported on Linux
SIGLWP	Ignore	Not supported on Linux
SIGFREEZE	Ignore	Not supported on Linux

Table 5.2 *(Continued)*

Signal	Solaris	Linux
SIGTHAW	Ignore	Not supported on Linux
SIGCANCEL	Ignore	Not supported on Linux
SIGRTMIN	Terminate	Not supported on Linux
SIGRTMAX	Terminate	Not supported on Linux

 This table is also available in the *Technical guide for porting applications from Solaris to Linux, Version 1.0.*[8]

5.4   RUNTIME LIBRARIES

A linker is responsible for linking the executables with the required shared libraries. Though both environments follow the same method for linking, there are some subtle differences (Table 5.3). Linux maintains two different sets of libraries: system libraries and user libraries. Solaris has only one set of libraries.

Table 5.3: Runtime Library Differences between Solaris and Linux

Function	Solaris	Linux
runtime linker	/usr/lib/ld.so.1	/lib/ld-linux.so.1
runtime linker configurator	**crle**	**ldconfig**

---

8. http://www.ibm.com/developerworks/eserver/articles/porting_linux/

Table 5.4: Filesystem Differences between Solaris and Linux

Filesystem	Solaris	Linux
Common filesystem	UFS	ext2/ext3
Journaling filesystems	Veritas	ext3, reiserfs
Filesystem for reading CDs	HSFS	iso9660
System information	PROCFS	proc
MS-DOS filesystem	PCFS	msdos or vfat

5.5   FILESYSTEMS

Migrating data from one filesystem to another can be accomplished either by data migration tools or by transferring the data over the network. Data transferring is the most time-consuming of the two. Linux has support for over thirty different filesystems, which are listed in the `mount(8)` manual page. In Solaris the predominant filesystem is UFS, in Linux it is ext2. Table 5.4 gives some filesystem differences between Linux and Solaris.

5.6   THREADS

Solaris provides a threading model under which all processes are based on threads called lightweight processes (LWP). In Solaris, a process will be associated with one or more LWPs. In the case of Linux, all threads are based on processes and each thread will be mapped to a process.

Solaris supports not only its native threading model but also the POSIX threading model; POSIX threads are also supported on Linux. If an application uses the Solaris native thread model then the application needs a lot of rework before it can be ported. If an application uses nonstandard proprietary functions, then the Solaris-compatible Thread Library (STL)[9] available on

9. `http://sourceforge.net/projects/sctl/`

Linux can be used to ease the migration of that application. This library provides the Solaris thread interfaces built upon the POSIX thread library.

5.7   ABSOLUTE ADDRESSES

Applications that use hard-coded addresses might be difficult to port. Some applications use `mmap()` calls for page fixing. Since each platform has its own way of handling the program stack, heap, system libraries, and so on, such a call to `mmap()` with a hard-coded address might result in a segment violation.

For instance, some addressing schemes ignore the high-order bits. So a hard-coded address of `0x80000000` might get translated to `0x00000000` and cause unintentional results. It is desirable to eliminate the usage of hard-coded addresses in the code. If an application mandates the use of hard-coded addresses, then it has to be changed to use only an allowed memory range, which you can obtain from `/proc/`*`application_pid`*`/map`.

5.8   PADDING

When a structure or an aggregate data type are used in the code, each platform has its own way of laying out the constituent elements. This arrangement is dependent on structure, architectural limitations, efficiency, and compiler. Most of the architectures cannot read data from odd addresses. Architectures such as PowerPC are inefficient in reading the data if it starts at an address not divisible by four. So, for efficiency purposes, compilers add the so-called *pad bytes*. The function of these bytes is to maintain byte alignment so that the code can perform efficiently.

On a 4-byte alignment platform, the compiler would lay out the structure in Example 5.6 as shown in Table 5.5, where P is padding, $d1_0$, $d1_1$ are bytes of d1, and $d2_{0-3}$ are bytes of d2.

In Table 5.5, the data structure occupies eight bytes because of the padding. On a platform that does not need any alignment, the compiler would lay out the same structure differently (Table 5.6).

Example 5.6: Pad Bytes

```
struct struct1{
   DATA2 d1;    // data of size 2 bytes
   DATA4 d2;    // data of size 4 bytes
}struct1;
```

Table 5.5: 4-Byte Alignment

$d1_0$	$d1_1$	P	P
$d2_0$	$d2_1$	$d2_2$	$d2_3$
. . .	. . .	. . .	. . .

Table 5.6: No Alignment

$d1_0$	$d1_1$	$d2_0$	$d2_1$
$d2_2$	$d2_3$	. . .	. . .
. . .	. . .	. . .	. . .

In Table 5.6, the data structure occupies only 6 bytes. If you are using functions such as sizeof() to measure the size of the structure, this behavior has to be taken into account while porting. Most compilers provide options for disabling or enabling byte alignment (including padding) that can be used if necessary, but disabling alignment will usually result in performance degradation.

5.9   TOOLSET

5.9.1   C/C++ Resources

On the Linux platform, the development tools are mostly those of the GNU Compiler Collection (GCC). GCC includes tools for both C and C++. GNU tools are also available for Solaris.[10] All Solaris applications can be first compiled with the GNU versions instead of the proprietary Solaris versions. However, the differences between the Solaris **make** utility and the GNU **make** utility (**gmake**) have to be resolved. The respective documentations can be used for this purpose. Once makefiles are made to work with **gmake**, rebuild the application. The errors thrown from a dry run with this makefile can be classified into command-line option errors and code errors. Command-line option errors are easy to resolve using Table 5.7 that contains the common options for the C compilers on Solaris and the GNU GCC (from *Technical Guide for Porting Applications from Solaris to Linux, Version 1.0*). For additional options, the respective compiler manuals should be used.

Table 5.7: Differences between Options for Sun Workshop and GCC

Sun Workshop	GCC	Description
-#	-v	Turn on verbose mode, showing each component as it is invoked.
-Xa	-ansi	Specify compliance with the ANSI/ISO standard. The GCC supports all ISO C89 programs. You can use -std to specify the particular version of ISO C.
-xinline	-finline-functions	Inline only those functions which are specified.
-xa	-ax	Generate extra code to write profile information for basic blocks, which will record the number of times each basic block is executed.
-xspace	-O0	Do not optimize.

10. http://www.sunfreeware.com/

Table 5.7 *(Continued)*

Sun Workshop	GCC	Description
`-xunroll=`	`-funroll_loops`	Perform the optimization of loop unrolling only for loops in which the number of iterations can be determined at compile time or run time.
`-xtarget=`*name*	`-b=`*machine*	The *machine* argument specifies the target machine for compilation. In addition, each of these target machine types can have its own special options, starting with m, to choose among various hardware models or configurations.
`-xo, -O`	`-O, -O1, -O2, -O3, -Os`	Control various sorts of optimizations.
`-xmaxopt`		Ensure that GCC does not use #pragma.
`-xnolib`	`-nostdlib`	Do not link any libraries by default.
`-fsingle`	`-fsingle-precision-constant`	Treat floating point constants as single precision constants instead of implicitly converting them to double precision.
`-C`	`-C`	Tell the preprocessor not to discard comments. Used with the `-E` option.
`-xtrigraphs`	`-trigraphs`	Support ISO C trigraphs.
`-E`	`-E`	Preprocess all the C source files specified and output the result to standard out or to the specified output file.
`-xM`	`-M`	Run only the preprocessor on the specified C programs, asking it to generate makefile dependencies and send the result to the standard out.

Table 5.7 *(Continued)*

Sun Workshop	*GCC*	*Description*
-xpg	-pg	Generate extra code to write profile information suitable for the **gprof** analysis program.
-c	-c	Direct the compiler to suppress linking with **ld** and to produce the .o file for each source file.
-o	-o	Specify the name the output file.
-S	-S	Direct **cc** to produce an assembly source file but not to assemble the program.
-xtemp	TMPDIR	Specify the directory to use for temporary files if the TMPDIR environment variable is set.
-xhelp=f	-help	Display online help information.
-xtime	-time	Report the CPU time taken by each subprocess in the compilation sequence.
-w	-q	Suppress compiler warnings.
-erroff=%none	-W	Display the warning messages.
-errwarn	-Werror	Treat all warnings as errors.

Errors could also be thrown from the linker (if code compilation was successful). The most common command-line options of the SPARCworks linker and the GNU linker are shown in Table 5.8 (from *Technical Guide for Porting Applications from Solaris to Linux, Version 1.0*).

The code-related error messages and warnings are mainly due to the difference in acceptable constructs and APIs semantics between the compilers. These errors should be resolved by referring to the compiler manuals.

Table 5.8: Differences between Options in SPARCworks and GNU Linkers

SPARCworks	*GNU gld*	*Description*
`-a`	`-static`	Enable the default behavior in the static mode and prevent linking with the shared libraries. The linker is creating an executable and undefined symbols cause error messages.
`-b`		Achieve the equivalent of the GNU linker by not compiling the source code with the options `-fPIC` or `-fpic`.
`-g`	`-g`	Produce debugging information in the operating system native format.
`-m`	`(-M)`	Print a linker map. The `-M` option prints something comparable but with a different format and slightly different content.
`-s`	`-S/-s`	Achieves the equivalent of the `-s` option by using `-S` with the GNU linker, which removes only the debugging information.
`-h` *name*	`-soname` *name*	Set *name* as the shared object name.
`-o` *filename*	`-o` *filename*	Place output in a file. This applies regardless of the type of output being produced. The default is to put an executable file in `a.out`.
`-L` *dir*	`-L`*dir*	Add directory *dir* to the list of directories.
`-R` *path*	`-rpath` *path*	Specify the search path for the runtime linker.

## PART III

Certifying for the LSB

LSB Certification program is essential for Linux-based runtime environments (distributions) and Linux-based application developers and vendors. It provides an assurance to users and customers that the certified software product has the highest possible runtime adherence to the LSB specifications. It provides a foundation that ensures that a certified application will work with any LSB-certified or LSB-compliant runtime environments.

Certification makes an LSB runtime environment and application more valuable to the consumer.

Day to day operations of the LSB Certification program are managed by an independent Certification Authority (CA). The Certification Authority manages the process of becoming certified and audits the submissions for certification. The LSB Certification program is not a profit center for the Free Standards Group. Prices are kept to a minimum to encourage developers, ISVs, and Linux distributions to become LSB-certified.

The following two chapters describe LSB Certification for runtime environments and applications, respectively. To become familiar with the LSB Certification program, you should read the following program documents available from the LSB Certification Web site (`http://www.opengroup.org/lsb/cert/`): The LSB Certification Policy, which covers the overriding policies of the program, and the LSB Product Standards, which contain the detailed conformance requirements for the different product types that can be certified.

## CHAPTER SIX

LSB Certification for Linux Distributions

This chapter provides an overview of LSB Certification for a runtime environment and is based on the Guide to LSB Certification (`http://www.opengroup.org/lsb/cert/docs/LSB_Certification_Guide.html`) produced by The Open Group. An overview of LSB Certification for application programs is provided in the next chapter.

6.1 INTRODUCTION

Products or ranges of products that meet the LSB conformance requirements can apply for LSB certification. The certification process requires a demonstration of conformance to the LSB Certification Authority (a vendor-neutral third party). The detailed requirements for conformance are identified in the LSB Product Standards and include passing sets of tests and completing a Conformance Statement. Only suppliers of certified products are permitted to use the LSB trademark in connection with their product.[1]

A number of documents contain the requirements of the LSB Certification program. The LSB Certification Policy governs the Free Standards Group LSB Certification program. The use of the LSB trademark is governed by the LSB Trademark License Agreement. The LSB Certification Agreement covers the

---

1. Portions of this chapter were derived with permission from LSB Certification, The Open Group (`http://www.opengroup.org/lsb/cert/`).

terms and conditions of the certification service. If you intend on submitting a product for certification then you must agree to the terms and conditions outlined in all three documents prior to certification.

6.1.1   Highlights

Significant highlights of the LSB certification process are outlined below:

- The LSB Certification program is administered on behalf of the Free Standards Group by its designated Certification Authority, The Open Group.

- Applicants will be granted a license to use the LSB trademark in connection with a product once the product has passed the applicable certification test suite(s) and the applicant has formally agreed to all the required terms.

- The LSB Trademark License Agreement must be fully signed (signatures are required from both the applicant and the Free Standards Group) in order to have a product certified.

- A certified product is subject to recertification on a periodic basis as stated in the LSB Certification Policy.

- All product information supplied to the Certification Authority will be treated as confidential, as required by the LSB Certification Agreement.

- The LSB Certification Authority may, from time to time, request proof that the certified product remains in compliance with the requirements outlined in the LSB conformance requirements, as required by the LSB Certification Policy.

6.2   ACHIEVING LSB CERTIFICATION

This section details the steps required to achieve certification and provides information on how to perform each of these steps. The process involves

- Understanding the certification program and process
- Testing the product informally

- Applying for certification
- Formal testing and submission of results

6.2.1   Understanding the Certification Program

To become familiar with the program, the following program documents should be read:

- LSB Certification Policy
- LSB Product Standards

6.2.1.1   LSB Certification Policy

It is best to start with the LSB Certification Policy, which is the foundation of the program. It provides information on what types of products can be certified in the program, what it means to be certified, what is required to get a product certified and how to make sure that a product remains certified. The LSB Certification Policy defines the following types of products:

- LSB Application
- LSB Runtime Environment
- LSB Internationalized Runtime Environment
- LSB Development Environment

The definitions of these products are included in Section 1, Overview, of the LSB Certification Policy.

 In the current version of the program, registrations are only being accepted for the first three of these product types.

6.2.1.2   LSB Product Standards

The LSB Product Standards should then be read to understand the detailed conformance requirements against which a product can be certified. Product standards provide a mapping between certification, the LSB specifications, and the test suites needed to demonstrate conformance. There is an LSB product standard for each type of product that can be certified. The LSB

Certification Web site should be consulted for the current set of product standards for which certifications are being processed.

In order to determine which product standards are suitable for a product to be certificied against, applicants should review Section 3, Conformance, of the LSB Certification Policy and the LSB Product Standards.

6.2.2   Confidentiality

The applicant's company and product details are confidential between them and the LSB Certification Authority. This is effective once the applicant accepts the LSB Certification Agreement, which is a prerequisite to registering a product. The Certification Authority does not make any certification information available to any third party, including Free Standards Group employees, consultants, or members, without the written permission of the applicant.

Upon successful completion of the certification process, the certified product will be included in the publicly available Certification Register.[2] However, to enable applicants to launch a certified product, they can request that their certification remain confidential for up to six months from the date of written notification by the Certification Authority that a product has achieved certification. A request that the certification remain confidential can be made in the final step of the product registration (see Section 6.3.7). See Section 11.3 of the LSB Certification Policy for further information.

6.2.3   Informal Testing

Normally, testing a product with the LSB certification test suite(s) is the first activity. Applicants should read the applicable product standard for the product that is being considered for certification, referring to the Indicators of Compliance section to identify the required certification test suites. These test suites are freely available from the Free Standards Group and should be used, along with any additional method deemed appropriate, to make sure that the product meets the applicable conformance requirements and is ready for entry into the certification program.

---

2. http://www.opengroup.org/lsb/cert/register.html

6.2.3.1 Authorized Test Suites

It should be noted that for formal testing, only currently authorized versions of the LSB certification test suites can be used. So, for informal testing it is vital that you use an authorized version. The Certification Authority maintains a list of the currently authorized certification test suites.[3] Since the test suites come from multiple sources, this online document includes information on how to obtain the test suites.

6.2.3.2 Problems and Problem Reporting

If problems are encountered when running the certification test suites, first read the documentation provided with the test suite. If this does not answer the questions, please check the Frequently Asked Questions.[4] If an answer still cannot be found, a report should be sent to the appropriate Test Suite Maintenance Authority as noted in the Frequently Asked Questions file.

If one of the authorized test suites is being used and failures occur but it is believed that the product conforms to the specifications, check the Problem Reporting[5] information database. The online Problem Reporting database contains known information on existing bugs and interpretations of the specification. The issue may already be resolved by an LSB Specification Interpretation, or by an agreed Test Suite Deficiency. If it is not, please submit a new problem report.

6.2.4 Certification

Certification is a formal process. The supplier of a certified product warrants and represents that the product meets all the conformance requirements applicable to the product standard against which it is certified, and implements all the features claimed in the Conformance Statement.

The obligations, terms, and conditions of certification are fully set out in the following documents:

---

3. http://www.opengroup.org/lsb/cert/docs/testsuites.html

4. http://www.opengroup.org/lsb/cert/docs/faq.html

5. http://www.opengroup.org/lsb/cert/PR/

- LSB Certification Policy
- LSB Trademark License Agreement
- LSB Certification Agreement

These documents are available from the LSB Certification Web site.[6] These documents should be read before the certification process is started in order to fully understand the policies and requirements.

6.2.5   The Trademark License Agreement

The LSB Trademark License Agreement (TMLA) is between the supplier and the Free Standards Group and requires signature. It is recommended that suppliers commence the process to complete the Trademark License Agreement as soon as possible to avoid delays later in the certification process. A trademark license must be obtained before a product can complete the certification process and be entered onto the Certification Register.

The Trademark License Agreement only needs to be entered into once per organization. When it is in place, multiple products can be certified.

6.2.6   The Certification Agreement

You are required to agree to the LSB Certification Agreement for each product registration. The LSB Certification Agreement is between the supplier and the Certification Authority. It defines the certification service and the legal commitment to the conditions of the service.

 The LSB Certification Agreement is a Web-based agreement. When suppliers click the **I accept** button they indicate that they accept the terms and conditions of the Agreement.

---

6. `http://www.opengroup.org/lsb/cert/`

6.3   PRODUCT REGISTRATION

6.3.1   The Trademark License Agreement

Although not required to be completed before commencing product registration, we recommend suppliers to submit a completed LSB Trademark License Agreement to the Free Standards Group as early as possible in the process.

6.3.2   The Conformance Statement

The next step is to complete a Conformance Statement to describe your product and how it meets the conformance requirements. A Conformance Statement will be linked to the Certification Register entry for the product once it is certified. A template Conformance Statement Questionnaire[7] is available for each product standard.

The LSB Certification Web site should be consulted for the list of the currently available Conformance Statement Questionnaires.

Suppliers must complete the relevant questionnaire to create a Conformance Statement for a product. See Sections 1.2, 2, and 3.3 of the LSB Certification Policy for further information on the purpose of the Conformance Statement.

Conformance Statement Questionnaires are provided as HTML templates. Suppliers should download the template and edit the HTML, retaining the existing layout. The completed Conformance Statement must then be submitted in HTML format to the Certification Authority using the Web certification system.

Conformance Statement Questionnaires have common frontmatter that asks for the following information about the company and the product being certified:

Submitter information   Organization name and the name of the author of the Conformance Statement.

---

7. http://www.opengroup.org/lsb/cert/docs/conformance.html

Product information   The name of the product and its unique version or release identifier.

Operation environment   The LSB processor-specific architecture with which the conformance of the product has been demonstrated.

Indicator(s) of compliance   The names and versions of the test suites used to demonstrate the conformance of the product.

The policy on rebranding of this product   This question allows the supplier to state their policy with respect to third parties rebranding and recertifying the product. Under an open rebranding policy, you can state here that you waive the LSB Certification Policy requirement that a written permission be given in this case. Otherwise, you might just want to indicate that the policy is as stated in the LSB Certification Policy.

The Conformance Statement Questionnaire also contains questions specific to a product standard.

6.3.3   Submitting Initial Certification Information

The LSB Certification Authority provides a Web certification system[8] through which products can be submitted for certification. Applying for certification requires the supplier to submit some initial information via the Web. The initial submission involves completing a registration form (including company details and contact details), and accepting the terms and conditions of the LSB Certification program. This only has to be done for the initial product registration.

Consult the Certification Authority Web site for further information on the process of registering for using the Web certification system.

---

8. `http://www.opengroup.org/lsb/cert/`

6.3.4   Registering Your Product within the Web Certification System

When a product is registered, a number of product details including the product name and the version or release for which conformance has been demonstrated have to be provided.

The supplier must select the LSB product standard against which certification is being sought, can optionally enter a product-related Web address, and then must accept the LSB Certification Agreement in order to proceed with this product registration.

The product registration form is then displayed with additional fields for you to provide information specific to a product standard as described in the following sections of this chapter.

6.3.4.1   LSB Runtime Specific Details

If a product is an LSB Runtime Environment, the supplier needs to answer to the following questions about the product.

- Select the languages that the product supports.
- Select the region where the product is targeted.
- Select the hardware profile that the product requires (minimum memory, processor type, minimum disk space, minimum processor speed).
- Select the usage profile that best matches the product (desktop/server/ cluster).

In several cases, multiple selections are allowed (for example, for the language and region). The responses to these questions will be published in the Certification Register.

6.3.4.2   LSB Internationalized Runtime Environment Specific Details

If the product is an LSB Internationalized Runtime Environment, you need only enter the product name since all other details are declared in the Conformance Statement.

6.3.5   Uploading Your Conformance Statement

The certification system leads suppliers through the steps required to register a product to be certified. The first document that must be uploaded to the certification system is the Conformance Statement for the product.

The next steps are to perform formal testing and then upload the test results as a sequence of files into the Web certification system.

6.3.6   Formal Testing for Certification

Formal testing is a self-test activity whose results are submitted to the Certification Authority for audit via the Web certification system. At this point in time you need to make sure you understand the required test campaign (Figure 6.1), that is, you must know which test suites are required to be used for certification testing (see the following paragraph for details). You also need to make sure that you have obtained the currently authorized version of the certification test suite(s), since other versions will not be valid for formal testing.

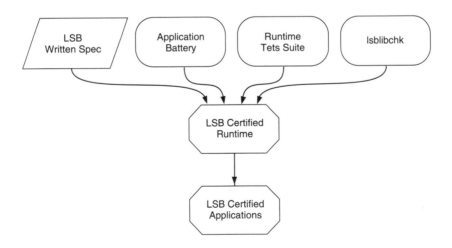

Figure 6.1: LSB Test Campaign

When a test campaign requires a warranty of the product working in a particular situation, or a warranty that selected applications execute correctly on the product, then a Web form will prompt for confirmation during the final registration stage. For any problems encountered, it will allow for a problem report ID to be referenced.

You can obtain help and information as described in Section 6.2.3.

6.3.6.1   Test Journals

Test results submitted should always include the full journal output from an uninterrupted run of the applicable test suite. If this is not possible, a problem report must be raised stating the nature of the problem and you should wait for a response from the Certification Authority before proceeding further.

Within the Web certification system you are required to upload test journals for each applicable test suite. The system also allows you to obtain a summary report of the result status for a test journal. If you decide that this test journal is your formal certification test run for your product, you must then select the validation tool within the Web certification system. This tool will automatically analyze the test results, and, if there are no failed test results or tests requiring manual resolution, then the journal will be flagged as OK in the system. If there are failed test results detected by the validation tool, then a screen will be presented to you with a list of test cases that you will need to resolve. If there are tests requiring manual resolution, a screen is also presented with a list of test cases you need to resolve.

The failed test results in the test journal that require resolution are those with a status of FAIL, UNINITIATED, UNRESOLVED, or UNREPORTED. The resolution process requires you to enter a valid reference to an approved problem report from the Problem Reporting database for each failed test case. An approved problem report is one that has resulted in an agreed Interpretation of the specification, a Test Suite Deficiency, or a Certification System Deficiency. These apply to specific releases of the specification, test suite, or certification system.

The test results in the journal that require manual resolution are denoted FIP (further information provided). The resolution process requires you to assert that the test case resolves to a PASS result for your system, and optionally to provide brief commentary. No reference is required to an approved problem report for `FIP` results.

6.3.6.2   *Test Campaign Definition*

For an initial certification a standard set of test campaigns are defined in the product standards. These are summarized in the following list:

LSB Runtime Environment

- The LSB Runtime Environment Conformance Statement must be completed.

- Test journal output (TET journal format required) from an uninterrupted run of the LSB Runtime Test Suite must be provided.

- Test journal output (TET journal format required) from an uninterrupted run of LSB library checker tool (**lsblibchk**) must be provided.

- For the test journal output, any `FAIL`, `UNRESOLVED`, `UNREPORTED`, or `UNINITIATED` results need to be resolved by referring to the associated granted Interpretations, Test Suite Deficiencies, or Certification System Deficiences, from the Problem Reporting database.

- For the test journal output, any `FIP` results need to be manually resolved to a `PASS` result.

- A list of the binary applications from the LSB Application Battery[9] that the applicant warrants work correctly must be provided (note that this declaration is provided in the Conformance Statement).

LSB Internationalized Runtime Environment

- The product must be already or concurrently registered as an LSB Runtime Environment.

- The LSB Internationalized Runtime Environment Conformance Statement must be completed.

---

9. `http://www.linuxbase.org/appbat/`

- Test journal output (TET journal format required) from an uninterrupted run of the LSB Internationalized Runtime Environment automated test suite must be provided.

- For the test journal output, any `FAIL`, `UNRESOLVED`, `UNREPORTED`, or `UNINITIATED` results need to be resolved by referring to the associated granted Interpretations, Test Suite Deficiencies, or Certification System Deficiences from the Problem Reporting database.

- For the test journal output, any `FIP` results need to be manually resolved to a `PASS` result.

- For the LSB Internationalized Runtime Environment, interactive validation procedures require completion of a self-assessment question-naire within the Web certification system. This requires you to manually assert for each set of test assertions within the interactive validation proce-dures that you pass the assertion, or reference a granted problem report.

For initial certifications, a complete run of the listed test tools is required for the product standards listed. For renewals and certification updates you should refer to the Certification Authority Web site for more information.

6.3.7   Confirming Your Submission

Once input of all the required information is complete, the Web certification system displays a form into which the final details are entered to submit a product for certification. This is done in two stages.

1. This form allows the supplier to check all the information relating to the company, the product, and the registration. It is divided into sections; each section needs confirmation that its content is correct. The form also includes an option to indicate that the registration must be kept confiden-tial prior to product launch. If any of the information needs correcting at this point, it can be updated.

2. The second and final part is to affirm the commitment to the terms and conditions of the program as stated in the LSB Trademark License Agreement and the LSB Certification Agreement. Certification fees[10] are

---

10. `http://www.opengroup.org/lsb/cert/docs/LSB_Fee_Schedule.html`

due at this stage. Please note that if a payment method other than by credit card is chosen, the submission cannot be processed until the payment is received by the Certification Authority.

6.3.8   Completion of Certification

If the submission is complete and an LSB Trademark License Agreement is in place, the supplier will be notified of successful certification within 15 calendar days. If for any reason the submission was not complete, the supplier will be notified so that any corrections can be made and resubmitted. Such a resubmission needs to be done within 60 calendar days unless an extension has been granted by the Certification Authority. The initial fee covers one set of corrective actions.

The details of the certified product will then be put on the Certification Register, which is a public document, unless it has been requested that the certification remains confidential. To keep the certification confidential, this option must be selected in the Web certification system at the time the product is submitted.

When a product certification has been made public, the supplier will be sent a certificate by electronic mail.

Certification is valid for a certain period as defined in Section 8.1, Duration of Certification, of the LSB Certification Policy. At the end of that period, if the supplier wishes the product to remain certified, the certification of the product will need to be renewed (see Section 6.4.1).

For the product standards, such as the LSB Internationalized Runtime Environment, that are built upon other product standards, the following rules apply. If registration is occurring at the same time as the other product standard, then the duration of certification is the shorter one of the two defined durations. Otherwise, if the registration references a preexisting product standard certification for the product, then the duration for the additional product standard ends on the end date associated with the existing certification.

6.3.9 Appeals Process

Suppliers may appeal decisions made by the Free Standards Group or the Certification Authority as stated in Section 10, Appeals Process, of the LSB Certification Policy. Any request for appeal should be sent by electronic mail to lsb-cert@opengroup.org. Receipt of such a request will be acknowledged within six working days by the Certification Authority and the appeals process will be invoked.

6.4 RENEWALS AND CERTIFIED PRODUCT UPDATES

6.4.1 The Renewals Process

A certified product has a defined duration of its initial certification, after which it must be renewed or the product will no longer be certified. The Certification Authority will notify the supplier about two months in advance by electronic mail when a renewal is due (it is important to keep contact information current). At any time, the supplier may use the Web certification system to obtain the renewal dates for certified products.

Renewal implies that the product continues to conform and that the supplier will continue to support the product for the duration of the renewal period. Consult the Certification Authority Web site for more information on renewal policy and on how renewals are undertaken.

6.4.2 Certified Product Updates

If any changes are made to a certified product, the supplier may be required to retest or recertify as required by Section 6, Scope of Certification and Requirements for Product Retest and Recertification, of the LSB Certification Policy. The supplier should read that section thoroughly since it describes multiple scenarios related to product changes, some of which require a certification-related activity. In some cases, a complete full certification is required since the update is equivalent to a new product so far as certification is concerned.

6.4.2.1   Maintenance Releases

If the change to a product qualifies as a maintenance release (as defined in Section 6.1, Maintenance Releases, of the LSB Certification Policy), the supplier is not required to contact the Certification Authority.

Suppliers may request an update to a product's certification information to include the maintenance release. Depending on how the maintenance release is described, this may be a wise thing to do so as to avoid marketplace confusion regarding which versions of the products are certified. Updates to the certification information of a product can be done by contacting the Certification Authority.

6.4.2.2   Renaming a Product

If a supplier decides to rename a certified product (as defined in Section 6.3, Renamed Products, of the LSB Certification Policy), they should contact the Certification Authority including the details of the required change and a written statement to the Certification Authority indicating that there have been no material changes to the certified product. The Certification Authority will change the product name on the Conformance Statement and in the Certification Register and issue a new certificate.

If a product is a submission in progress and has not yet been submitted for audit to the Certification Authority, then renaming the product can be done using the Web certification system.

6.4.2.3   Rebranding a Certified Product

If a supplier wants to rebrand a product (as defined in Section 6.4, Re-branded Products, of the LSB Certification Policy), they should locate and read the Conformance Statement for that product to obtain information on the product supplier's policy with respect to rebranding. First, the supplier should find out whether they have the permission required for rebranding. Then they proceed into the Web certification system as if they were certifying a new product, except that when asked to input information about the product, they should select that this is a rebranded product.

The main difference between a rebranded product registration and a new product registration is that no test results are required to be submitted.

Upon submission, the Certification Authority will verify that a supplier has permission.

6.4.2.4   Other Scenarios

Other scenarios are treated as new products and are subject to full certification.

6.5   CURRENTLY SUPPORTED SYSTEMS

The LSB is one of the most successful ABI standards in the history of the Information Technology industry. Every major GNU/Linux distribution is LSB-certified, and LSB conformance testing has become a staple of quality assurance for everyone concerned. A current list of LSB-certified distributions and applications can be found on the LSB Web site.[11]

6.5.1   Summary of Web References

A summary of the external Web references is given below:

- The starting point for Free Standards Group Certification[12]
- The LSB Certification Policy[13]
- The LSB Application Battery[14]
- The OpenI18N specifications[15]
- The LSB Written Specification[16]

---

11. http://www.linuxbase.org/test/registered.html

12. http://www.freestandards.org/certification/

13. http://www.opengroup.org/lsb/cert/docs/LSB_Certification_Policy.html

14. http://www.linuxbase.org/appbat/

15. http://www.openi18n.org/

16. http://www.linuxbase.org/spec/

- The starting point for the LSB Web certification system[17]
- The Guide to LSB Certification[18]
- The LSB Certification Register[19]
- The current set of LSB Product Standards[20]
- The list of currently authorized LSB Test Suites[21]
- The Problem Reporting database[22]
- The Frequently Asked Questions file[23]
- The Conformance Statement Questionnaires[24]

---

17. http://www.opengroup.org/lsb/cert/

18. http://www.opengroup.org/lsb/cert/docs/LSB_Certification_ Guide.html

19. http://www.opengroup.org/lsb/cert/register.html

20. http://www.opengroup.org/lsb/cert/docs/prodstandards.html

21. http://www.opengroup.org/lsb/cert/docs/testsuites.html

22. http://www.opengroup.org/lsb/cert/PR/

23. http://www.opengroup.org/lsb/cert/docs/faq.html

24. http://www.opengroup.org/lsb/cert/docs/conformance.html

## CHAPTER SEVEN

LSB Certification
for Software Products

This chapter provides an overview of LSB Certification for application programs and is based on the Guide to LSB Certification (`http://www.opengroup.org/lsb/cert/`) produced by The Open Group.

7.1 INTRODUCTION

Products or ranges of products that meet the LSB conformance requirements can apply for LSB certification. The certification process requires a demonstration of conformance to the LSB Certification Authority (a vendor-neutral third party). The detailed requirements for conformance are identified in the LSB Product Standards, and include passing sets of tests and completing a Conformance Statement. Only suppliers of certified products are permitted to use the LSB trademark in connection with their product.[1]

---

1. Portions of this chapter were derived with permission from LSB Certification, The Open Group (`http://www.opengroup.org/lsb/cert/`).

7.1.1   Highlights

Significant highlights of the LSB certification process are outlined below:

- The LSB Certification program is administered on behalf of the Free Standards Group by its designated Certification Authority, The Open Group.

- Applicants will be granted a license to use the LSB trademark in connection with a product once the product has passed the applicable certification test suite(s) and the applicant has formally agreed to all the required terms.

- The LSB Trademark License Agreement must be fully signed (signatures are required from both the applicant and the Free Standards Group) in order to have a product certified.

- A certified product is subject to recertification on a periodic basis as stated in the LSB Certification Policy.

- All product information supplied to the Certification Authority will be treated as confidential, as required by the LSB Certification Agreement.

- The LSB Certification Authority may, from time to time, request proof that the certified product remains in compliance with the requirements outlined in the LSB conformance requirements, as required by the LSB Certification Policy.

7.2   ACHIEVING LSB APPLICATION CERTIFICATION

This section lists the steps required to achieve LSB Application certification, and provides information on how to perform each of these steps. The process involves:

- Understanding the certification program and process
- Testing the product informally
- Applying for certification
- Formal testing and submission of results

7.2.1   Understanding the Certification Program

To become familiar with the program, the following program documents should be read:

- LSB Certification Policy
- LSB Product Standards

7.2.1.1   LSB Certification Policy

The LSB Certification Policy document covers more than just LSB Application certification. However, it provides information on what it means to be certified, what is required to get a product certified, and how to make sure that a product remains certified. It states:

> "LSB Application certification is for applications conforming to the LSB specifications. LSB applications are the consumers of the services provided by LSB Runtime Environments."

7.2.1.2   LSB Product Standards

The LSB Product Standards should be read to understand the detailed conformance requirements against which a product can be certified. The Certification Authority Web site should be consulted for the current set of product standards that LSB Application products can be certified against.

7.2.2   Informal Testing

Normally testing a product with the LSB certification test suite(s) is the first activity. The Indicators of Compliance section of each product standard identifies the required certification test suites. These test suites are freely available from the Free Standards Group and should be used, along with any additional method deemed appropriate, to make sure that the product meets the applicable conformance requirements and is ready for entry into the LSB Certification program.

7.2.2.1   Guidelines for an LSB-Certified Application

The following list of guidelines will help you decide whether or not an application can be certified as illustrated in Figure 7.1. A compliant application has at least the following properties:

- Only relies on LSB-specified interfaces to be provided by the runtime environment it executes on (see Section 13.3.3)

- Is linked against the LSB runtime linker and LSB stub libraries, or versions of libraries that by default provide LSB versions of interfaces for linking against (see Section 13.3.1)

- Either statically links non-LSB libraries, or bundles the shared libraries with the application

- Passes the **lsbappchk** test (see Section 13.5.2)

- Is FHS-compliant (see below)

- Passes the functional verification testing on the LSB Sample Implementation and two other LSB-compliant systems (see Section 12.3)

- Is packaged in the RPMv3 format (with the restrictions as outlined in the specification) or uses an installer that is LSB-compliant itself (see Section 4.1)

FHS compliance

For LSB certification, applications must conform to the Filesystem Hierarchy Standard. During the certification process there is the following FHS questionnaire to be answered:

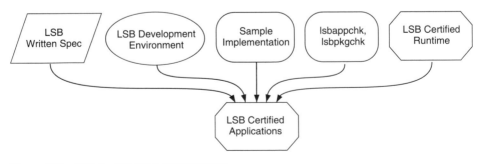

Figure 7.1: LSB Application Certification

- Is the application installed into /opt/*package*/ or /opt/*provider*/?

- Is the application to be invoked by the end user via the library installed into /opt/*package*/bin/ or /opt/*provider*/bin/?

- Are the man pages of the application installed in /opt/*package*/man/ or /opt/*provider*/man/?

- Are the variable files of the application created in /var/opt/*package*/ or /var/opt/*provider*/?

- Are the host-specific configuration files of the application kept in /etc/opt/?

- Are there other package files that reside outside /opt/, /var/opt/, and /etc/opt/ (e.g., /var/lock/ or /var/run/)?

7.2.2.2   Authorized Test Suites

It should be noted that, for formal testing for LSB Application certification, only currently authorized versions of the LSB certification test suites can be used. So, for informal testing it is vital that an authorized version is also used to avoid later problems. The Certification Authority maintains a list of the currently authorized certification test suites.[2] Since the test suites come from multiple sources, this online document includes information on how to obtain the test suites.

7.2.3   Registering an LSB Application Product within the Web Certification System

The LSB Application certification uses the same Web certification system as for the LSB Runtime Environment certification. For brevity, we include an overview in this chapter detailing the differences of LSB Application certification. See also Chapter 6 for more details on a Conformance Statement, product amendments, and renewals that apply equally to LSB Application certification.

---

2. http://www.opengroup.org/lsb/cert/docs/testsuites.html

When a product is registered, a number of product details have to be provided, including the product name and the version or release for which conformance has been demonstrated.

The supplier must select the LSB product standard against which certification is being sought, then optionally enter a product-related Web address. The LSB Certification Agreement must be accepted in order to proceed with this product registration.

The product registration form is then displayed with additional fields for the supplier to provide the product standard specific information described below.

LSB Application Specific Details.   For an LSB Application, the supplier needs to warrant and demonstrate that the product executes correctly in a number of environments. The first of these environments is the LSB Sample Implementation. Secondly, the product needs to run correctly on two different LSB Runtime Environments, of which one can be chosen by the supplier and the other is selected by the Certification Authority.

Suppliers are required to make their own arrangements to obtain the LSB Runtime Environments for testing. The Certification Authority is unable to provide assistance other than the contact information on the Certification Register. The Free Standards Group may be able to assist with obtaining a runtime environment.

At the final stage of registering a product within the Web certification system, a form requires a declaration that the supplier warrants and has demonstrated that the application executes correctly in the required environments.

7.2.4   Uploading a Conformance Statement

The Web certification system will lead the supplier through the steps to register a product to be certified. The first document that must be uploaded to the certification system is the Conformance Statement for the product.

The next steps are to perform formal testing and then upload the test results as a sequence of files into the Web certification system.

7.2.5   Formal Testing for LSB Application Certification

Formal testing is a self-test activity whose results are submitted to the Certification Authority for audit, via the Web certification system. Only authorized test tools are valid for certification.

When a test campaign requires the warranty of the product working in a particular situation, or the warranty that selected applications execute correctly on the product, then a Web form will prompt for confirmation of that during the final registration stage and allow for a problem report ID to be referenced for any problems encountered.

7.2.5.1   Test Journals

Test results submitted should always include the full journal output from an uninterrupted run of the applicable test suite. If this is not possible, a problem report must be raised stating the nature of the problem and a response received from the Certification Authority before proceeding further.

Within the Web certification system, the supplier is required to upload test journals for each applicable test suite. The system also allows the supplier to obtain a summary report of the result status for a test journal. If this test journal is the formal certification test run for a product, the supplier must select the validation tool within the Web certification system. This will then automatically analyze the test results, and if there are no failed test results or tests requiring manual resolution, then the journal will be flagged as OK in the system. If there are failed test results detected by the validation tool, then a screen will be presented with a list of test cases that need to be resolved.

In the test journal, the failed test results that require resolution are those with a status of FAIL, UNINITIATED, UNRESOLVED, or UNREPORTED. The resolution process requires the supplier to enter a valid reference to an approved problem report from the Problem Reporting database for each failed test case. An approved problem report is one that has resulted in an agreed Interpretation of the specification, a Test Suite Deficiency, or a Certification System Deficiency. Each of these applies to a specific release of the specification, test suite, or certification system.

7.2.5.2   *Test Campaign Definition*

For an initial certification, the following standard set of test campaigns is defined in the product standards:

LSB Application

• Warranty that the application executes correctly on the two selected LSB Runtime Environments and the LSB Sample Implementation must be provided.

• The LSB Application Conformance Statement must be completed.

• Test journal output (TET journal format required) from an uninterrupted run of the LSB application checker tool (**lsbappchk**) must be provided. (This can be the execution of **lsbappchk** against the product on either the LSB Sample Implementation, or one of the two selected LSB Runtime Environments).

• For the test journal, any `FAIL`, `UNRESOLVED`, `UNREPORTED`, or `UNINITIATED` results need to be resolved by reference to associated granted Interpretations, Test Suite Deficiencies, or Certification System Deficiences from the Problem Reporting database.

For initial certifications a complete run of the listed test tools is required for the product standards listed. For renewals and certification updates you should refer to Section 4, Renewals and Product Updates, of the Guide to LSB Certification for information on the applicable test campaigns.

7.2.6   Completion of Certification

If the submission is complete and an LSB Trademark License Agreement is in place, the supplier will be notified of successful certification within 15 calendar days. If for any reason the submission was not complete, the supplier will be notified so that any corrections can be made and resubmitted. Such a resubmission needs to be done within 60 calendar days unless an extension has been granted by the Certification Authority. The initial fee covers one set of corrective actions.

The details of the certified product will then be put on the Certification Register, which is a public document, unless it has been requested that it remains confidential. To keep the certification confidential, this option must be selected in the Web certification system at the time the product is submitted.

When a product certification has been made public, the supplier will be sent a certificate by electronic mail.

Certification is valid for a defined period as stated in Section 8.1, Duration of Certification, of the LSB Certification Policy. At the end of that period, if the supplier wishes the product to remain certified, the product certification will need to be renewed.

7.3   CURRENTLY SUPPORTED SYSTEMS

The LSB is one of the most successful ABI standards in the history of the Information Technology industry. Every major GNU/Linux distribution is LSB-certified and LSB conformance testing has become a staple of quality assurance for everyone concerned. A current list of LSB-certified distributions and applications can be found on the LSB Web site.[3]

7.3.1   Summary of Web References

A summary of the external Web references is given below:

- The starting point for Free Standards Group Certification[4]
- The LSB Certification Policy [5]
- The LSB Application Battery[6]
- The OpenI18N specifications[7]

---

3. http://www.linuxbase.org/test/registered.html

4. http://www.freestandards.org/certification/

5. http://www.opengroup.org/lsb/cert/docs/LSB_Certification_Policy.html

6. http://www.linuxbase.org/appbat/

7. http://www.openi18n.org/

- The LSB Written Specification[8]
- The starting point for the LSB Web certification system[9]
- The Guide to LSB Certification[10]
- The LSB Certification Register[11]
- The current set of LSB Product Standards[12]
- The list of currently authorized LSB Test Suites[13]
- The Problem Reporting database[14]
- The Frequently Asked Questions file[15]
- The Conformance Statement Questionnaires[16]

---

8. http://www.linuxbase.org/spec/

9. http://www.opengroup.org/lsb/cert/

10. http://www.opengroup.org/lsb/cert/docs/LSB_Certification_
Guide.html

11. http://www.opengroup.org/lsb/cert/register.html

12. http://www.opengroup.org/lsb/cert/docs/prodstandards.html

13. http://www.opengroup.org/lsb/cert/docs/testsuites.html

14. http://www.opengroup.org/lsb/cert/PR/

15. http://www.opengroup.org/lsb/cert/docs/faq.html

16. http://www.opengroup.org/lsb/cert/docs/conformance.html

## PART IV

Contributing to the LSB Project

The LSB Written Specification is by no means static. The specification will expand in scope according to acceptable requirements. Future enhancements will increase the sophistication of the LSB and confidence in applications resulting in improved market opportunities.

Progress of the LSB in adding new architectures and ABIs to the specification is dependent on staff, volunteers, and sponsorships. The following chapters describe the acceptance criteria and process by which the specification can be expanded. Your requirements, comments, and contributions are welcomed.

## CHAPTER EIGHT

Adding New Interfaces to the LSB Written Specification

This chapter describes the process by which the LSB workgroup and Open Source community expands the standards by adding new interfaces to the LSB Written Specification.

8.1   MOVING FORWARD

As mentioned in previous chapters, the first few years of the LSB efforts and the initial versions of the specifications produced in those years were the product of a core group of Linux developers with a closely shared vision. As that vision matured and both the specification and audience grew, it became clear that a more formal process was needed. No longer could everyone using and developing the LSB be expected to have internalized this vision, so an official process needed to be created. The process used in the early years served its purpose of quickly identifying the "low-hanging fruit" that needed to go into the core specification right away, and tolerance for minor mistakes was a worthwhile trade-off for an accelerated schedule. However, once the first official version of the Written Specification was released June 2001, the audience of the standard was now much larger and was demanding both a high quality, stable standard and additional new interfaces. A group of people interested in these goals began meeting on a regular basis to discuss them. This group of people became the LSB Futures subcommittee `<lsb-futures@freestandards.org>` of the LSB workgroup. In addition to tracking new interfaces, the group developed the official criteria and processes for adding new interfaces.

The LSB effort is unique in that it is standardizing interfaces that were developed (or endorsed in implementation) by the Free/Libre and Open Source Software (FLOSS) communities. Most previous standardization efforts were the result of industry consortiums that could often dictate the direction of the standard, despite dissenting voices. This is not to say that previous standards efforts did not try to build consensus among those involved, only that the LSB effort represents a consensus on a scale not seen before. Where previous efforts could make standardization choices based on primarily technical factors, release a new version of a standard, and expect implementors to make changes to match the new specification, the LSB workgroup must hold to a different model. First, consensus about the interface must be built among the community, then the interface must be implemented among the major runtime providers, and finally, and only after those steps are completed, can it be added to the LSB Written Specification. As a method of objectively measuring these steps, a list of selection criteria was created.

8.2   LSB Selection Criteria

Candidates for inclusion in the LSB, via the LSB Futures process, progress by completing a series of steps divided into three broad categories: *identification*, *investigation*, and *implementation*. The first two are informational, and progress is made by supplying the information for tracking. If there are no blocks in these phases, the implementation phase can commence.

8.2.1   Phase 1: Identification

Demand   There needs to be sufficient demand for the component to be standardized. Demand can be measured in many ways, such as heavy usage of a component in the community or multiple requests from developers. Keep in mind that, while there may be demand for many things, not all will meet the additional criteria.

License   The component should have at least one compliant implementation available under an open source license that also promotes a "no strings attached" environment for developers. This means that the developers would be able to develop and deploy their software however they choose using at least one standard implementation. This is interpreted to mean that at least one implementation is available under a license that meets the Open Source Definition, but also does not restrict proprietary usage at runtime or in development. The rationale for this criteria is very similar to that of licenses like the LGPL: By licensing under terms that allow use by all programs, the interface can be put into much wider use.

Best Practice   The candidate must represent the "best practice" in the development community for the problem it solves. It needs to have emerged as a clear de facto standard and be available on most (or all) of the major distributions.

Stable ABI/API   The API/ABI is required to be stable enough to target for standardization. The maintainers need to follow the "best practices" for ABI/API stability; they should have a proven track record for doing so, and properly resolving any issues that arise.

Dependencies Present   The candidate's runtime dependencies should either already exist in the LSB, or be planned to be added, or be abstracted away so that specifying their interfaces is not required. Dependencies provide an insight into things that may need to be added and/or potential problems that may be encountered. Recursive dependencies should be listed and discussed before proceeding.

8.2.2   Phase 2: Investigation

Upstream Cooperative   The upstream maintainers must be committed to backwards compatibility (for some defined version) and stability. They should be willing to work with developers and distributors on providing a standard everyone can agree on and adopt.

Distribution Maintainers Cooperative   The component maintainers for the distributors should be willing to work together. They should be willing to work with upstream maintainers and developers on providing a standard everyone can agree on and adopt.

Component Versions   The upstream maintainers, distributions, and developers should be synced up on compatible versions. If not, they should be willing to agree on and adopt compatible versions.

Distribution patches   If the distributions maintain any patches against the component, these could be merged upstream or dropped. Since the LSB is a behavioral standard, this is not required but could make things easier.

Internationalization   If the component interacts with the user it should, if possible, have internationalization (i18n) support and support localization (l10n) as appropriate. The lack of a specific locale's data should be remedied in a timely manner, although it is admittedly hard to support every locale.

Resources   Resources for working on the deliverables required in Phase 3 should be arranged. A component may be an excellent candidate for standardization but can't proceed until there are people to do the work. Depending on the candidate, there may be parties who would benefit from the standardization and could reasonably be asked to contribute to the effort.

Rationale   The rationale for why the component needs to be added should be recorded and published. Mailing lists and meeting minutes are not sufficient; this data needs to be recorded in the specification or in a separate document. Lack of rationale documentation has already been a problem with older versions of the specification, so this is very important.

8.2.3   Phase 3: Implementation

Import into LSB Database   Importing the component into the LSB database is a first step for working on the LSB Written Specification, Runtime Test Suites, Development Environment, and Sample Implementation.

Written Specification   Development or adaptation of the Written Specification for that component must be done in the proper format for integration into the LSB Written Specification.

Initial Test Suite   Development or adaptation of the test suites for that component must be done in the proper format for integration into the LSB Test Suites.

Development Components   If required the source for the stub libraries and header files for that component must be created, in the proper format, for integration into the LSB Development Environment. For simple components, these may simply be used as a cross-check against the database generated header files found in the LSB Development Environment.

Sample Implementation   The sample binaries for that component are then built, in the proper format for integration into the LSB Sample Implementation.

Application Battery   If suitable, this step should provide a recommendation of a reasonable application that uses the component for inclusion into the Application Battery.

8.2.4   Final Steps

Once a candidate has completed all three phases, the LSB Futures subcommittee will recommend it to the LSB workgroup for inclusion in the next version of the LSB. The items completed in Phase 3 will be transitioned to the Written Specification, Test, Development Environment, Sample Implementation, and Application Battery subcommittees.

8.3   CANDIDATE IDENTIFICATION

As its name implies, one of the jobs of the LSB Futures subcommittee is to identify where the LSB should go in the future. This means identifying new candidate ABIs for consideration for inclusion in the standard. Several methods have been identified and used in this process.

8.3.1   Input from Specification Audience

By far the largest and most important source of new candidates is the suggestions from the LSB standards audience. Given the huge number of Linux developers, there are many ideas for interfaces the developers would like to see in the standard. The LSB Futures subcommittee solicits these suggestions, gathers, and organizes them. This organization helps to clarify suggestions (often several people suggest the same thing, but in different ways) and gauge the level of demand for an interface.

8.3.2   Analysis of Existing Code

In addition to the input directly from Linux developers, several methods have been identified to programmatically determine the interfaces most in demand by developers.

Linux distribution dependencies   By examining packaging dependencies of the major distributions, we can make guesses at what interfaces are most often depended on. These packages might be good candidates for standardization.

Linux distribution base components   The packages that major distributions include in their "base install" are important and represent the collective wisdom of the users and maintainers of the distribution. These packages might be good candidates for standardization. A large portion of the packages in a base system are the things that make a distribution unique, but the things that don't fall into that category are often common across distributions and are therefore good candidates.

Existing commercial application dependencies   By examining existing commercial application binaries it can be determined what interfaces they depend on and what other system features they expect to have available.

8.3.3   Standards Ideas

The previously mentioned methods are good for identifying library interfaces but are rarely helpful in identifying other things about the system that would benefit from standardization. The LSB Futures subcommittee also spends time brainstorming ideas for standards to solve these types of problems.

Some examples are additions to the Filesystem Hierarchy Standard, system services for applications to use, restructuring the standard, and helping to determine when subgroups need to be formed to investigate a new area.

8.4 CANDIDATE TRACKING

In the previous sections the LSB criteria and methods for identifying potential candidates were described. Using those, the LSB Futures subcommittee tracks the status of the proposed candidates on a publicly browsable Web page.[1]

For each candidate, its status with respect to meeting each of the LSB selection criteria is listed along with some additional tracking data and an overall summary. This makes it easy to see what work needs to be done for a particular candidate. As mentioned in the criteria section, once a candidate has met all the criteria, it can be added to the next version of the LSB Written Specification.

One nice thing about this tracking system is that it allows for *any* potential candidate to be added; if that candidate can meet the criteria, then it belongs in the LSB. Sometimes a candidate will be added but will be blocked as being unable to meet certain parts of the criteria. It continues to be tracked, and if and when it can meet the criteria then it can be added. It makes the process more objective and protects against things being added before they are ready.

8.5 PROBLEM CASES

In the course of tracking candidates, the LSB Futures subcommittee has encountered a few classes of candidates that, while in demand, are problematic to add. The following sections describe a few examples of this.

8.5.1 Linux Specific Requests

One of the most requested categories of interfaces are those that are related to the Linux kernel. In particular, developers would love to have a kernel

---

1. http://www.linuxbase.org/futures/candidates/

module API. This is problematic for two main reasons. The first is that it fails the criteria that requires support of the upstream developer. The Linux kernel community has explicitly stated that they will not commit to an ongoing standard interface because they want to be able to change that interface as needed when it makes sense. The second reason is that the LSB has yet to define anything kernel-related and would prefer to keep it that way in order to not preclude runtime implementations on non-Linux systems.

8.5.2   Interpreted Languages

Another common request is for interpreted languages such as Perl, Python, and Tcl/Tk. The main reason that these are currently blocked is the lack of a formal standard that the LSB can reference. Most of these languages have stable interfaces, what's needed is a formal specification that the upstream maintainer will stand behind.

8.5.3   License Issues

Some candidates fail to meet the LSB license criteria due to the fact that the only existing implementation is under a license, such as the GPL, that requires anyone using that interface to also release the source code to their software. The LSB seeks to maximize the numbers of people using free standards and FLOSS. The license criteria was selected as a way of providing a "no strings attached" environment. If the only viable implementation of an interface is licensed under the GPL or a similar license, then the LSB would become less appealing to those not willing to use restrictive licenses. This is essentially the argument for the existence of licenses such as the LGPL, whose terms allow the use by all programs so that the interface can be put into much wider use.

For example, the LSB Futures subcommittee is tracking two windowing toolkits, GTK+ and Qt. GTK+ is currently proceeding as it is licensed under the LGPL and requires the normal efforts to be added to the Written Specification. Qt, on the other hand, is currently blocked since the only implementation is covered by a dual license, either QPL (GPL terms, requires release of source) or commercial. This has generated quite a bit of discussion on the mailing list. Qt continues to be tracked, and if an implementation that meets the license criteria becomes available, it will be unblocked and can proceed.

8.6   HOW TO GET YOUR FAVORITE INTERFACE ADDED TO THE LSB

The LSB processes are designed to not get in the way of people wanting to contribute. If you have a candidate that you would like to see added to the standard, you can request that it be tracked as a candidate. If the work gets done to make the candidate fulfill the criteria, then it can be added. The only thing limiting when something can be added to the LSB is how quickly the criteria can be fulfilled. The LSB workgroup would love to see additional interfaces added and encourages all to participate.

## CHAPTER NINE

Adding New Architectures to the LSB Portfolio

This chapter describes the process by which the LSB workgroup added new architectures to the LSB Written Specification portfolio.

9.1   ARCHITECTURE-SPECIFIC SUPPLEMENT

The LSB is composed of two basic parts: a common specification ("generic LSB" or "gLSB") describing those parts of the interface that remain constant across all implementations of the LSB, and an architecture-specific specification ("archLSB") describing the parts of the interface that vary by processor architecture. Together, the generic LSB and the architecture-specific supplement for a single hardware architecture provide a complete interface specification for compiled application programs on systems that share a common hardware architecture.

The architecture-specific supplement must be used in conjunction with the generic LSB. It provides architecture-specific information that supplements the generic LSB, as well as additional information that is not found in the generic LSB. Listed below are several components of the LSB that are architecturally specific:

- Executable and Linking Format (ELF)
- Library symbol versions
- Header file data structures

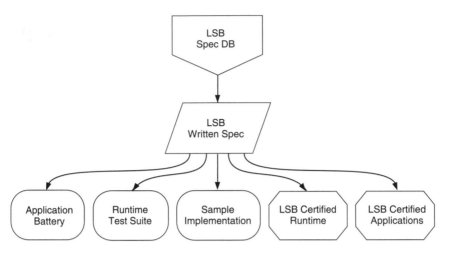

Figure 9.1: LSB Database

- Architecture-specific attributes of RPM packaging
- Sample Implementation

This chapter will briefly describe how the LSB imports and cross-checks new architecture-specific ABIs.

9.2   ARCHITECTURE-SPECIFIC ELF

ELF defines the linking interfaces for compiled application programs. The LSB has a database containing most of the ELF specifics for Linux. The LSB database (Figure 9.1) is what is used to build the Written Specification and the LSB tools.

9.3   ARCHITECTURE-SPECIFIC SYMBOL VERSIONS

Library stability for applications is maintained on Linux by the use of symbol versioning. If an ABI changes, then a copy of the ABI is created with a new symbol version. Previously built applications continue using the interfaces they were originally linked to, and recently linked applications will use the latest ABIs.

For LSB compliance, the existence of common symbol versions in system libraries is checked using the LSB library checker tool **lsblibchk** (Example 9.1). New or changed symbol versions are discovered when running **lsblibchk**. Architecturally differing ABI symbol versions are grouped in the LSB ABI. The common set of architecture symbols in the LSB ABI are what applications need to be binary compatible to.

Example 9.1: Using **lsblibchk**

```
# rpm -i lsblibchk-2.0.0-1.i385.rpm
# /opt/lsblibchk/bin/lsblibchk
```

9.4 ARCHITECTURE-SPECIFIC HEADERS

In the LSB Development Environment, the LSB provides Linux header files according to the LSB Written Specification (Example 9.2). These header files are *ifdef*-ed for architectural differences only. Using the LSB header files for compilation dramatically improves binary compatibility for applications.

Example 9.2: Installing LSB Header Files

```
# rpm -i lsb-build-base-2.0.0-1.i486.rpm
# /bin/ls /opt/lsbdev-base/include
```

A Linux header files runtime can be checked using **lsbdevchk**.

9.5 ARCHITECTURE-SPECIFIC PACKAGING

Application RPMs are packaged according to architecture. For example, the package `lsb-pkgchk-2.0.0-1.i486.rpm` has been compiled and packaged for an Intel 486 or better system. The LSB package verification tool

can be used to check the architecture and generic correctness of a package
(Example 9.3).

Example 9.3: Package Verification

```
# rpm -i lsb-pkgchk-2.0.0-1.i486.rpm
# /opt/lsb/bin/lsbpkgchk lsb-xpdf-1.01-3.i486.rpm
```

9.6   ARCHITECTURE-SPECIFIC SAMPLE IMPLEMENTATION

The LSB Sample Implementation is a minimal LSB-conforming runtime environment used for testing purposes. Architectural anomalies are discovered
during the process of building the toolchain and the functional areas of the
LSB. For detailed information, see Section 12.4.

9.7   ARCHITECTURAL CHECKLIST

Before a new LSB architectural specification can be released, it must satisfy a
list of prerequisites. Before an LSB architectural specification candidate can
be submitted to the Free Standards Group for approval, the following items
must be completed and beta-tested:

- Architecture specification
- Runtime conformance tests
- Runtime library checker (**lsblibchk**)
- Application Battery
- Development Environment
- Sample Implementation
- Application checker (**lsbappchk**)
- Two or more Linux Implementations readily available

As an example of applying the checklist, the architecture specification for
LSB 1.3 for the PPC64 architecture was submitted by the LSB to the FSG for

approval, then released. At that time, there was an existing implementation. It seemed that all the necessary work had been done. However, later it emerged that this implementation had chosen to apply architecture support in a way that did not completely match what some of the upstream maintainers were doing, and other implementations intended to follow the upstream. One example was **glibc** symbol versions, which were different from those in the upstream **glibc**. In August 2003, the LSB was forced to rescind the PPC64 specification (it was resubmitted for LSB 2.0) on the grounds that architecture support had not yet matured enough. In the future, the "two or more implementations" rule will be used to avoid this sort of problem. Luckily, there were no LSB-certified Linux distributions nor LSB-certified applications for this platform.

## PART V

Using LSB Resources

The LSB is not your ordinary specification. The LSB also provides a test suite to validate the conformance to the Specification and a Sample Implementation to demonstrate the specification and validate the tests. A well-tested and illustrated Written Specification increases confidence in its validity and reduces anomalies and omissions.

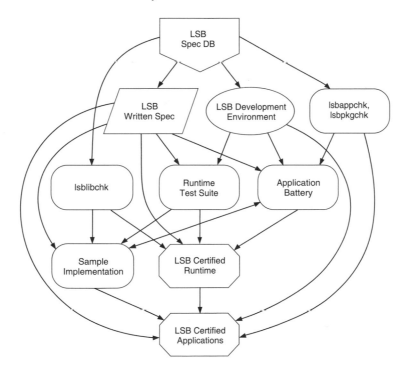

CHAPTER TEN

Using the LSB Written Specification

This chapter describes what the LSB Written Specification is used for and what it is not intended to be used for.

10.1 UNDERSTANDING THE LSB WRITTEN SPECIFICATION

The LSB Written Specification comprises a set of documents specifying a binary compatibility environment. The documents are structured along hardware architectures, with the common material supported on all architectures in a single document called the generic specification (known as gLSB or LSB-Core) and then one additional supplementary document for each supported architecture. For LSB 2.0, the generic specification is modularized into a series of options to enable support for smaller footprint devices and to allow devices to not support all the options if they are not needed in a specific marketplace.

Instead of duplicating the descriptions of interfaces that are standardized by other groups such as the IEEE POSIX standards and The Open Group Single UNIX Specification, the LSB references a number of published standards and specifications. Other examples of referenced documents include the OpenGL Application Binary Interface for Linux document for the OpenGL, the appropriate ELF specifications, and the System V Interface Definition (SVID).

For each of the interfaces in these libraries, there is a specification of the interface behavior, the ABI it presents, and, where applicable, the symbol version. To reduce duplication and the chance of editing errors, references are made to a description in one of the base standards, or sometimes a reference plus a small difference (for example, "for the LSB, the -g option is also allowed"). The LSB provides a full description only when a reference specification is not found.

The LSB also defines a standard packaging format to allow portable installation of applications. The packaging format specified is a subset of RPMv3. Although packages of this format must be able to install on a compliant runtime (distribution), this does not mandate the use of the **rpm** program or database. For example, Debian-based distributions, which use the .deb format, can use programs such as **alien** to convert and install LSB-compliant software. Some features, such as trigger scripts, were not included; currently these cannot be supported nor converted easily to other packaging formats.

A number of utilities are included in the specification. For many of these, the behavior has already been defined by a POSIX specification. The gLSB documents cases where the behavior of the command on Linux diverges from this specification or it is a Linux-specific command. The criteria for selecting the commands to be included in the specification is their usefulness for scripts used for application installation, configuration, and basic maintenance.

The LSB also mandates a layout of the file tree by referencing the Filesystem Hierarchy Standard. In the area of system initialization, the LSB introduces some new concepts for init scripts. Historically, it has been difficult to automatically determine at what stage of the boot sequence a service should be started. LSB-compliant init scripts specify what services they provide and what they depend on. Thus, the system initialization service of the runtime is able to determine at what point to start or stop a service.

It is important to note that it is not required that the LSB Written Specification be only implementable on Linux-based systems. The intent is to allow for other operating systems to be able to present an LSB-compliant runtime environment to applications.

10.2 PRODUCT STANDARD DESCRIPTIONS

A *product standard* is a concise statement identifying those parts of the LSB Written Specification that must be implemented in a product carrying the LSB brand.

LSB Runtime Environment   The *LSB Runtime Environment for IA32* (or other architectures) product standard is for platforms providing services that conform to the LSB specifications, specifically the LSB 2.0 common specification (knows as gLSB or LSB-Core), in conjunction with the LSB specification for the IA32 (or other architectures) Architecture 2.0 processor-specific supplement (knows as archLSB or LSB-Core-IA32). For more details, see Section 6.3.4.1.

LSB Application   The *LSB Application for IA32* (or other architectures) product standard is for applications conforming to the LSB specifications, specifically the LSB 2.0 common specification (knows as gLSB or LSB-Core), in conjunction with the LSB specification for the IA32 (or other architectures) Architecture 2.0 processor-specific specification (knows as archLSB or LSB-Core-IA32). LSB Applications are the consumers of services provided by the LSB Runtime Environments. For more details, see Section 7.2.

10.3 SPECIFICATION MODULE DESCRIPTIONS

A *specification module* is a unique collection of one or more functions that have value for a certain group of runtime implementations. To borrow a business term, a specification module is specific to a "vertical market." Specification modules can range from informal concepts to certified standards. Product standards contain one or more of the following specification modules.

LSB-Core   Is a set of interfaces for developers targeting any general purpose Linux runtime. This includes only the basics for runtime environments.

LSB-Graphics   Provides graphics interfaces such as the X Window System libraries and the OpenGL library. It is to be used in conjunction with the LSB-Core module.

LSB-Embedded   Is minimal set of interfaces that a developer targeting an embedded system would expect to be able to find. This specification module is not currently included in any product standard, but can be added to one if there is demand. In addition, this module currently includes some things that may not be present in a version used for a product standard.

LSB-OpenI18N   Provides additional internationalization commands and interfaces beyond what is included in the LSB-Core. It is to be used in conjunction with the LSB-Core module.

10.4   FUNCTIONAL AREA DESCRIPTIONS

A *functional area* corresponds to the smallest standards unit with reasonable justification for individual existence. To divide it into smaller units would not make sense since implementors of that interface would implement all the smaller units anyway. Often the justification for a functional area will be the possibility that it will be useful for implementors who are targeting only some portions of the available standards in an *a la carte* manner.

Executable and Linking Format (ELF)   Is the definition of the executable files produced by the C compilation system.

Execution Environment   Consists of the filesystem hierarchy, minimal granted directory and file permissions, recommendations for applications on ownership and permissions, regular expression localization, filename globbing localization, and miscellaneous API behaviors.

Base Libraries   Consists of **libc**, **libm**, **libpthread**, **libgcc_s**, **libdl**, **libcrypt**, **libpam**, and **libstdcxx**.

Utility Libraries   Consists of **libz**, **libncurses**, and **libutil**.

System Initialization   Consists of **cron** jobs, init script actions, installation, and removal of init.d files.

Packaging   Consists of the RPM file format, script restrictions, package naming, package dependencies, and package architecture considerations.

Graphics   Consists of **libX11, libXext, libSM, libICE, libXt,** and **libGL.**

10.5 SPECIFICATION AMALGAMATION

Figure 10.1 is a visual representation of the new structure of the LSB. Each box represents a functional area. Functional areas are grouped according to the workgroup that maintains them: ELF, FHS, LSB, or Desktop. Functional areas are stacked according to their dependencies. The dimension arrows indicate what functional areas in the stack are included in a specification module.

Product standards, such as the LSB Runtime Environment, contain one or more specification modules such as the LSB-Core.

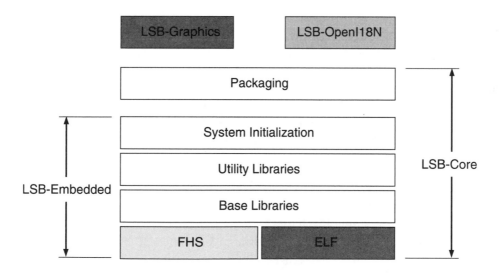

Figure 10.1: LSB Functional Areas and Specification Modules

10.6   EXPANDING THE LSB WRITTEN SPECIFICATION

Below are some of the acceptance criteria taken from Section 8.2 for publishing or revising an LSB Written Specification.

- The candidate must represent the "best practice" in the development community for the problem it solves. It needs to have emerged as a clear de facto standard and be available on most (or all) of the major distributions.

- The upstream maintainers must be committed to backwards compatibility (for some defined version) and stability. They should be willing to work with developers and distributors on providing a standard everyone can agree on and adopt.

- The upstream maintainers, distributions, and developers should be synced up on compatible versions. If not, they should be willing to agree on and adopt compatible versions.

- If the distributions maintain any patches against the component, these could be merged upstream or dropped. Since the LSB is a behavioral standard, this is not required but could make things easier.

Explicitly check the upstream support; a checklist item for supporting a new architecture should be an explicit check of the upstream components to ensure that the correct symbol versions are specified.

A validation step must be completed prior to a specification being approved by the LSB workgroup. This validation step consists of the completion of all components of the LSB Written Specification, Test Suites, Development Environment, Sample Implementation, and Application Battery. Our process is a closed loop when all of these components are in place.

Multiple implementations should exist and have been used in the validation step. If only a single implementation exists, then the LSB is not really needed, since no compatibility problem can exist. The LSB brand is intended for use by multiple vendors and distributions, and not as a marketing tool for a single vendor or distribution.

10.7   DOWNLOADING THE LSB WRITTEN SPECIFICATION

To obtain the LSB Written Specification go to the LSB Download Web page.[1] You can obtain the specifications in Adobe Portable Document Format (`.pdf`), RichText Format (`.rtf`), text (`.txt`), or line-numbered text (`_lines.txt`). Table 10.1 represents the information that can be accessed via the World Wide Web.

Table 10.1: LSB Written Specification Modules

Document	Version
LSB-Core	2.0
LSB-Core-AMD64	2.0
LSB-Core-IA32	2.0
LSB-Core-IA64	2.0
LSB-Core-PPC32	2.0
LSB-Core-PPC64	2.0
LSB-Core-S390	2.0
LSB-Core-S390X	2.0
LSB-Embedded	2.0
LSB-Graphics	2.0

•

1. http://www.linuxbase.org/spec/

## CHAPTER ELEVEN

Using the LSB Test Suites

This chapter describes the LSB Test Suites, how to obtain them, how to use them, and how to add more conformance tests.

11.1 UNDERSTANDING THE LSB TEST SUITES

The LSB Test Suites are a family of test suites for testing various aspects of the LSB. They include tests supplied in RPM format for testing LSB Runtime Environments for conformance to the LSB Written Specification. The tests are built in the LSB Development Environment to ensure they are LSB-conformant.

The test suites include both TET-based and non-TET-based tests. The Test Environment Toolkit (TET) is a framework and application program interface for test generation. The following sections describes each test.

11.1.1 TET-Based Tests

11.1.1.1 `lsb-runtime-test`

This test program is made up of a number of separate test modules combined into a single binary RPM.

POSIX.1–1990 test suite   Runtime tests for compliance against the POSIX.1–1990 standard.

LSB-OS test suite   Runtime tests for compliance of Linux-specific interfaces as defined in the LSB Written Specification and other interfaces from POSIX and the Single UNIX Specification required by the LSB Written Specification but not covered by the POSIX.1–1990 test suite.

FHS test suite   Tests for compliance against the FHS specification.

LSB Users/Groups test suites   Tests for compliance against the user and group components of the LSB Written Specification (commands and compulsory users and groups).

VSTH-lite test suite   A test suite for a subset of pThreads—POSIX 1003.1–1996 threads.

The utility tests are a separate standalone test suite:

VSC-lite test suite   Tests commands and utilities from POSIX 10003.2–1992.

11.1.1.2   `lsb-test-pam`

This is a binary version of the LSB pluggable authentication module (PAM) test suite. The PAM abstracts the mechanics of authentication from the application and enables the local system administrator to choose how individual applications will authenticate users. Header file tests from the test suites were removed.

11.1.1.3   `lsb-test-vsw4`

The X Window tests are a separate standalone test suite:

VSW4 test suite   Test suite for the X Window System, based on the MIT X Test Suite 1.2.

11.1.2   Non-TET-Based Tests

lsblibchk   A program that looks for LSB libraries and checks that those libraries contain the symbols required by the specification. If it is required that a symbol be versioned, then it checks that the symbol with the correct version exists in the library. This program can also be used for checking either the LSB Runtime Environment or the LSB Development Environment.

The rest of this chapter will discuss how to build and execute the tests and how to interpret test results for both TET-based and non-TET-based tests.

11.2   USING TET-BASED TESTS

This section will discuss how to install, build, and run the TET-based tests in `lsb-runtime-test`. It will also help you understand how to interpret the results of these tests. Figure 11.1 shows the inputs and outputs of the `lsb-runtime-test`.

11.2.1   Directory Hierarchy Description

All of the directory paths described are relative to $TET_ROOT, which is commonly `/home/tet`. The following list gives an overview of how the test cases fit together.

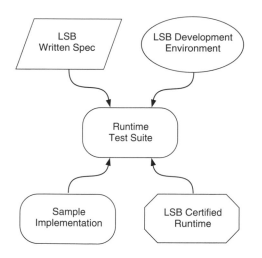

Figure 11.1: Runtime Test Suite

`/src`   Contains the TET framework source.

`/include`   Contains TET include files.

`/bin`   Contains TET framework binaries.

`/test_sets/tset`   Contains the source code for individual test cases. The directory hierarchy under this point is reflected in the `scen.bld` and `scen.exec` files that tell TET/VSXgen which test cases to build and run.

`/test_sets/TESTROOT/tset`   Contains a copy of the hierarchy under `/test_sets/tset`. This directory is automatically constructed and populated when the test suites are built.

`/test_sets/MAN/tset`   Contains a structure identical to `/test_sets/ tset` and the manual pages for individual test cases. These manual pages correspond to the test assertions. This information is useful for debugging test case failures.

`/test_sets/scripts`   Contains scripts supplied in the test suite tarballs that are used during the installation and configuration of the test suite. Scripts here are also supplied with the binary package to set up the correct environment prior to executing the test cases.

`/test_sets/results`   Contains journal files recording the results of building and executing the test cases. Directories ending in "b" contain build results, those ending in "e" contain execution results.

`/test_sets/SRC/common`   Contains library code. Some library code is supplied by VSXgen, and some is specific to a test suite.

`MAN/tset`   Contains documentation.

`SRC/subset`   Contains test set code.

`tsetscripts/`*`test_suite_name`*   Contains scripts that are run at suitable times during the setup and installation of the test suites.

11.2.2   Installing `lsb-runtime-test`

This section explains how to install the binary and source version of `lsb-runtime-test`. When you are installing `lsb-runtime-test` you should always check the beta versions of the packages to see if any bugs you have encountered have been fixed.

 In addition to the requirements specified by the LSB Written Specification, the following applications must also be installed for the tests to run correctly:

- **pax**
- Perl 5.x (only required for optional **tjreport** script)

11.2.2.1   *Installing the Binary* `lsb-runtime-test`

Complete the following steps to install the binary version of `lsb-runtime-test`.

All test suite files are available on the LSB Download Web site.[1]

1. Download the binary RPM.
2. Install the RPM:

```
# rpm -i lsb-runtime-test-version.architecture.rpm
```

11.2.3   Running `lsb-runtime-test`

Complete the following steps to run `lsb-runtime-test`.

1. Log out and log in as the user `vsx0`. You may need to first set the password for this account as it is not set to anything during the installation of the package.

---

1. `http://www.linuxbase.org/download/`

If you su to the user `vsx0` instead of logging in, then some tests will fail (such as those that verify that the tty is owned by the user who is logged in).

2. Execute `run_tests`:

   ```
   vsx0$ ./run_tests
   ```

3. View the journal file in the `/home/tet/test_sets/results/0001e/journal` directory.

   Example 11.1 shows how to run `lsb-runtime-test`.

Example 11.1: Running `lsb-runtime-test`

```
vsx0@rockhopper~$ run_tests
Name of person running tests (Automated)? IMA Testing
Organization (NONE)? LSB TSMA
Test System (Automated)? Your Runtime
Does the implementation provide bash as /bin/sh..? [y]
Does the implementation provide a C shell..? [y]
Enter the name of the Kernel (typically vmlinuz)..? [vmlinuz]
Does the implementation allow users to create devices using MAKEDEV..? [n] y
Does the implementation support process accounting..? [n]
Does the implementation support NIS..? [n]
/dev/loop0
Setting up loopback device
Enter the root password:
Password: ******
-----------------------------------------------------------------
Executing the test suites
It is not unusual for these test suites to take several hours to run.
tcc: journal file is /home/tet/test_sets/results/0001e/journal
11:46:13  Execute /tset/ANSI.os/charhandle/Misalnum/T.isalnum
11:46:14  Execute /tset/ANSI.os/charhandle/Misalpha/T.isalpha
11:46:15  Execute /tset/ANSI.os/charhandle/Miscntrl/T.iscntrl
11:46:17  Execute /tset/ANSI.os/charhandle/Misdigit/T.isdigit
11:46:18  Execute /tset/ANSI.os/charhandle/Misgraph/T.isgraph
...
```

11.2.4   Interpreting TET-Based Test Results

This section will help you understand how TET-based test results map to passing or failing.

11.2.4.1   Understanding TET Result Codes

Executing test cases will result in the creation of journal files. The result codes from the test cases are found in the journal files in `/home/tet/test_sets/ results/`*xxxx*`/journal`, where *xxxx* is a four-digit number starting at `0001` that is increased with each test suite run. Results of test case compilations are placed in journal files in a similarly named directory except ending in "b" instead of "e". Result codes are found in the following journal files:

`vrpt`   The **vrpt** will generate a report detailing all of the test cases executed and the result. There are several result types that can be separated into two main groups, `PASS` or `FAIL`; see below for result classification. For test cases that did not pass, the test assertion and test strategy will also be output.

`tjreport`   The binary test suites are also supplied with the **tjreport** tool. This will produce a summary of all the test cases run and the results, or optionally only display those that failed. It can also be used to intelligently compare two journal files and display those test cases whose results differ between the two test runs.

Raw journal files   If you want to interpret raw journal files manually, see Appendix C of the TETware User Guide.[2] This guide describes the format of the file.

The following lists explain the passing and failing result codes for TET.

Passing result codes

`PASS`   The test has been executed correctly and to completion without any kind of problem.

`WARNING`   The functionality is acceptable, but you should be aware that later revisions of the relevant standards or specifications may change the requirements in this area.

`FIP`   Additional information is provided, which needs to be checked manually. `FIP` results occur when, by default, the test suite is

---

2. `http://tetworks.opengroup.org/documents/3.3/uguide.pdf`

unable to determine whether a result is a PASS or FAIL. For LSB Certification you have to sign these off as resolving to PASS when you submit your test results into the Web certification system.

UNSUPPORTED   An optional feature is not available or not supported in the implementation being tested.

NOTINUSE   Some tests may not be required in certain test modes. Also, when an interface can be implemented by a macro or function and there are two versions of the test, only one is used.

UNTESTED   No test is written to check a particular feature, or an optional facility is needed to perform a test which is not available on the system.

Failing test codes   The following result codes are considered to be a fail for compliance testing purposes (unless the failure has been waived by an agreed problem report in the Problem Reporting database).

FAIL   The interface did not behave as expected.

UNINITIATED   The particular test in question did not start to execute.

UNRESOLVED   The test started but did not reach the point where the test was able to report success or failure.

UNREPORTED   A major error occurred during the testset execution.

 For these result codes, F stands for *function*, and M stands for *macro*. The operating system testset driver automatically generates tests for the macro version of each interface in addition to the underlying function. In general, not many function interfaces are implemented as macros, hence the high NOTINUSE count in that column.

11.2.5 Debugging TET-Based Test Suites

This section explains how to analyze test failures in the TET-based test suites. There is also additional TET documentation available.[3]

The following list explains some general debugging hints:

- The `in_rpt()` call works similarly to `printf()` and the output is put into the journal file.

- Edit the makefile for the test case (it is in the same directory as the code for the test case), and add debugging flags to the compile line.

- Many of the tests fork and execute the test code in the child, or have some form of communication with the parent. It can be useful to add `sleep()` calls in places to make it easier to attach with a debugger (especially when **gdb** is resisting following forks).

- It is often useful to write a small standalone program, using the test case code as a guide, that attempts to do the same things as the test. It helps to isolate implementation problems from test case and test harness problems and can be easier to debug. Also upstream maintainers will appreciate (if not insist on) having an easily compilable and executable test program when fixing bugs.

11.2.5.1 Setting Up the Debugging Environment

To set up the environment for debugging TET-based test suites, you must log in as the user `vsx0` and dot in the profile file in the `vsx0` home directory as follows:

```
vsx0$ . profile
```

 There is a limited amount of analysis that can be done with the binary versions of the test suites alone, as they are compiled without debug symbols.

---

3. `http://tetworks.opengroup.org/documents/docs33.html`

You can also enable some debugging information to be output during the execution of the tests by editing the file `/home/tet/test_sets/TESTROOT/tetexec.cfg`. This script automates the standard build and setup procedure for TET and VSXgen. Edit the setting for `VSX_DBUG_FLAGS` as follows:

```
VSX_DBUG_FLAGS=t:d,trace:1,2
```

The setting `VSX_DBUG_FILE` in the same file specifies where the debug information is placed. With reference to the source code for the test suite, it's often possible to work out the code path executed. The source tarballs are available on the LSB Download Web site.[4]

11.2.5.2   Debugging Individual Test Cases

This section explains how to debug individual test cases with and without the **tcc** (test case controller) command.

Debugging individual test cases with tcc.   If you only want to debug individual test cases, you can save time by not using the script for build and setup. You can execute individual test cases for debugging using one of the following **tcc** commands:

vsx0$ `tcc  -e` The `tcc  -e` command works similarly manner to the `tcc  -b` command but in executing test cases. This command will execute all of the test cases.

vsx0$ `tcc  -e  T.fgetpos` This command will execute only the `T.fgetpos` test.

The `tcc  -b` (build mode) and `tcc  -e` (execute mode) are shell functions that call **tcc**. You can find out more details on the uses of **tcc** in Chapter 6 of the TETware User Guide.[5]

For information on debugging individual test cases without **tcc**, see Section 11.2.5.4.

---

4. `http://www.linuxbase.org/download/`

5. `http://tetworks.opengroup.org/documents/3.3/uguide.pdf`

11.2.5.3   *Rebuilding and Executing Test Cases*

Once the TET/VSXgen framework has been configured and built you can (re)build and (re)execute any or all of the test cases. The file `/home/tet/test_sets/scen.bld` specifies the test cases that will be built and `/home/tet/test_sets/scen.exec` specifies those that will be executed.

Example 11.2 shows how to execute specific test cases by editing the `scen.bld` and `scen.exec` files. Before editing the files, you should back up both of them.

Example 11.2: Editing `scen.bld` and `scen.exec` to Execute Specific Test Cases

Before editing, both files appear as follows:

```
/tset/ANSI.os/charhandle/isalnum/T.isalnum
/tset/ANSI.os/genuts/strtod_X/T.strtod_X
/tset/ANSI.os/genuts/strtol_X/T.strtol_X
/tset/ANSI.os/genuts/system_X/T.system_X
/tset/ANSI.os/jump/longjmp/T.longjmp
/tset/ANSI.os/jump/setjmp/T.setjmp
/tset/ANSI.os/locale/setlocale/T.setlocale
/tset/ANSI.os/maths/acos/T.acos
/tset/ANSI.os/streamio/setbuf/T.setbuf
/tset/ANSI.os/streamio/tmpfile/T.tmpfile
/tset/ANSI.os/streamio/tmpnam/T.tmpnam
/tset/LI18NUX2K.L1/utils/od/od.sh
/tset/LI18NUX2K.L1/utils/wc/wc.sh
/tset/LI18NUX2K.L1/utils/cpio-fh/cpio-fh.sh
/tset/LI18NUX2K.L1/utils/find/find.sh
/tset/LSB.fhs/root/bin/bin-tc.sh
/tset/LSB.fhs/root/boot/boot-tc.sh
/tset/LSB.fhs/root/dev/dev-tc.sh
/tset/LSB.fhs/root/sbin/sbin-tc.sh
/tset/LSB.fhs/root/srv/srv-tc.sh
/tset/LSB.fhs/root/tmp/tmp-tc.sh
/tset/LSB.fhs/usr/x11r6/x11r6-tc.sh
/tset/LSB.fhs/usr/x386/x386-tc.sh
/tset/LSB.fhs/usr/bin/bin-tc.sh
/tset/LSB.fhs/usr/include/include-tc.sh
/tset/LSB.fhs/var/lib/lib-tc.sh
/tset/LSB.fhs/var/lib-misc/lib-misc-tc.sh
/tset/LSB.fhs/var/lock/lock-tc.sh
/tset/LSB.fhs/var/log/log-tc.sh
/tset/LSB.fhs/var/mail/mail-tc.sh
/tset/LSB.fhs/var/opt/opt-tc.sh
/tset/LSB.fhs/linux/var-spool-cron/var-spool-cron-tc.sh
/tset/LSB.os/aio/aio_cancel/T.aio_cancel
```

```
/tset/LSB.os/aio/lio_listio/T.lio_listio
/tset/LSB.os/aio/lio_listio_X/T.lio_listio_X
/tset/LSB.os/devclass/grantpt_L/T.grantpt_L
/tset/LSB.os/devclass/ptsname_L/T.pstname_L
/tset/LSB.os/files/dev_null/T.dev_null
/tset/LSB.os/files/dev_tty/T.dev_tty
/tset/LSB.os/files/seekdir/T.seekdir
/tset/LSB.os/files/telldir/T.telldir
/tset/LSB.os/files/telldir_L/T.telldir_L
/tset/LSB.os/genuts/closelog_L/T.closelog_L
/tset/LSB.os/genuts/fnmatch/T.fnmatch
/tset/LSB.os/genuts/ftw/T.ftw
/tset/LSB.os/genuts/wordexp/T.wordexp
/tset/LSB.os/streamio/fgetpos/T.fgetpos
/tset/LSB.os/streamio/fsetpos/T.fsetpos
/tset/LSB.os/string/mblen/T.mblen
/tset/LSB.os/string/mblen_L/T.mblen_L
/tset/LSB.os/string/mbstowcs/T.mbstowcs
/tset/LSB.os/string/memmove/T.memmove
```

After editing, both files appear as follows:

```
/tset/LSB.fhs/root/bin/bin-tc.sh
/tset/LSB.fhs/root/boot/boot-tc.sh
/tset/LSB.fhs/root/dev/dev-tc.sh
/tset/LSB.fhs/root/sbin/sbin-tc.sh
/tset/LSB.fhs/root/srv/srv-tc.sh
/tset/LSB.fhs/root/tmp/tmp-tc.sh
/tset/LSB.fhs/usr/x11r6/x11r6-tc.sh
/tset/LSB.fhs/usr/x386/x386-tc.sh
/tset/LSB.fhs/usr/bin/bin-tc.sh
/tset/LSB.fhs/usr/include/include-tc.sh
/tset/LSB.fhs/var/lib/lib-tc.sh
/tset/LSB.fhs/var/lib-misc/lib-misc-tc.sh
/tset/LSB.fhs/var/lock/lock-tc.sh
/tset/LSB.fhs/var/log/log-tc.sh
/tset/LSB.fhs/var/mail/mail-tc.sh
/tset/LSB.fhs/var/opt/opt-tc.sh
/tset/LSB.fhs/linux/var-spool-cron/var-spool-cron-tc.sh
```

11.2.5.4   *Executing Test Binaries Directly*

It can sometimes be useful to execute test binaries directly (for example, if you want an easier way to attach a debugger). Although the source for the test cases is located in the /home/tet/test_sets/tset, when they are built, the binaries are placed under an identical directory hierarchy under /home/tet/test_sets/TESTROOT/tset.

To run test binaries directly, complete the following steps:

1. Log in as vsx0.

2. Set the following environment variables:

   ```
   vsx0$ export TET_CONFIG=$TET_EXECUTE/tetexec.cfg
   vsx0$ export TET_CODE=$HOME/tet_code
   ```

3. Change to the directory containing the test case and run the executable. A journal file will not be created, but the contents of what would have been placed in the journal file for that test will be left in tet_xres in the current directory.

11.2.5.5   Executing a Single Test Case

The lowest level of granularity in the lsb-runtime test allows you to execute individual tests. Most tests can be executed in this way, but some are dependent upon execution of earlier tests in the testset, in which case only groups of dependent tests may be executed as a single unit.

The **tcc** can perform a one-off execution of selected test cases from a single testset. For example, to run test cases 3, 7, and 8 from the T.write test case in the POSIX.os category, use the following command:

```
vsx0$ tcc -e -l /tset/POSIX.os/ioprim/write/T.write{3,7,8}
```

11.2.5.6   Running Only the Tests That Failed

To execute testsets that failed during a previous run, use the following command:

```
vsx0$ tcc -e -r code-list other-options old-journal-file
```

The code-list is a comma-separated list of result codes to be reexecuted. The other-options are the other **tcc** options (for example, -y or -n). The old-journal-file is the journal file the codes are extracted from. For example, to reexecute all the tests that failed with FAIL, UNRESOLVED, and UNINITIATED codes from journal file results/0002e/journal, use the following commands:

```
vsx0$ cd results

vsx0$ tcc -e -r FAIL,UNRESOLVED,UNINITIATED \
-s ../scen.exec 0002e/journal
```

11.2.6   Installing the Source of `lsb-runtime-test`

Complete the following steps to install the source version of `lsb-runtime-test`.

All test suite files are available on the LSB Download Web site.[6]

1. Download the source RPM.

2. Install the RPM:

   ```
   # rpm -i lsb-runtime-test-version.src.rpm
   ```

3. Copy the file `lsb-runtime-tests-version.tar.gz` to the `/home/tet` directory (or the directory where you want to install the test suite):

   ```
   # cp lsb-runtime-tests-version.tar.gz /home/tet
   ```

4. Untar the file:

   ```
   tar xvfz lsb-runtime-tests-version.tar.gz
   ```

5. Run `install.sh` from the directory where you unpacked the files:

   ```
   # ./install.sh
   ```

   The license information for all of the packages you installed is displayed followed by instructions on how to proceed further.

6. Log out and log in as the user `vsx0`. You may need to first set the password for this account as it is not set to anything during the installation of the package.

7. Build the test harness by running `/home/tet/setup.sh`:

   ```
   vsx0$ ./setup.sh
   ```

---

6. `http://www.linuxbase.org/download/`

If you want to install additional test suites, unpack the tarball for that test suite in /home/tet/test_sets as the user vsx0 and run the setup script again.

11.2.7   Configuring lsb-runtime-test

To configure lsb-runtime-test, follow the on-screen instructions and answer the questions to fit your testing scenario. Example 11.3 shows the questions and answers for the default testing scenario.

Example 11.3: Default Testing Scenario

```
Setup loopback disk? [y]
Enter loopback device to use [/dev/loop0]
Run config.sh ..? [y]
Which test mode do you require
(from: POSIX96 UNIX98) [UNIX98]?
What is your name [Unknown]?
What is the agency for whom you are running VSX [Unknown]?
What is the system on which you are running VSX [Unknown]?
Where is the root directory of the tree from which the
testsets will be executed [/home/tet/test_sets/TESTROOT]?
How fast is your machine (1=very fast, 10=slow) [5]?
The system include directories (in order of searching) are:
      /usr/include
Is this correct (y/n) [y]?
What is your C compiler called (must be c89 for
UNIX98 registration runs) [/usr/bin/cc]?
What command line options does your C compiler need [-ansi]?
What link editor options does your C compiler need [none]?
Searching for archive maintenance tools ...
There are no additional libraries needed to compile VSX
Is this correct (y/n) [y]?
Using C compiler to establish understanding of type "long double"
*** Compiler supports type "long double"
What command line options does your C compiler need, instead of the normal
options, when compiling thread-safe programs [none]?
Which library is your maths library [-lm]?
(should be of form: -l<name> or full pathname):
What is the mountable device to be used for ENOSPC testing [/dev/loop0]?
Producing a new parameter file in /home/tet/test_sets/SRC/vsxparams
```

The default values for the configuration questions are those used for the build of the binary versions of the test suites. If you believe that a setting is wrong for the platform you are testing please send an email to `lsb-test@freestandards.org`.

For more information on running `lsb-runtime-test`, see Section 11.2.3.

11.2.8   Building `lsb-runtime-test`

You can build the `lsb-runtime-test` using the **tcc** command.

To build all of the test cases, use the following command:

```
vsx0$ tcc -b
```

The names of the test cases are displayed as they are built, but build failures are not shown. You should inspect the journal file to see any failures, especially if you have changed the test case code.

You can also use the **tcc** command to build a subset of the available test cases. The following examples show two different ways to use the `tcc -b` command to do this.

`vsx0$ tcc -b T.fgetpos`   Builds `/tset/LSB.os/streamio/fgetpos/ T.fgetpos` from the `lsb-os` test suite.

`vsx0$ tcc -b string`   Builds the following test cases from the `lsb-os` test suite:

- `/tset/LSB.os/string/mblen/T.mblen`
- `/tset/LSB.os/string/mblen_L/T.mblen_L`
- `/tset/LSB.os/string/memmove/T.memmove`
- `/tset/LSB.os/string/wcstombs/T.wcstombs`
- `/tset/LSB.os/string/wctomb/T.wctomb`

11.3 USING NON-TET-BASED TESTS

11.3.1 Using lsblibchk

The **lsblibchk** verifies whether the runtime system libraries for the current system appear to conform to the LSB. The **lsblibchk** checks the object format, whether all of the required libraries are present, whether the libraries contain all interfaces required by the LSB, and whether the interfaces have the symbol versions required by the LSB. The **lsblibchk** then prints warnings for any problems.

You can also use **lsblibchk** to check only the libraries in a specific module using the -M flag.

11.3.1.1 Installing *lsblibchk*

To install the binary RPM package for **lsblibchk**, complete the following steps.

1. Download the package from http://www.linuxbase.org/download/.

2. Install the binary RPM package:

   ```
   # rpm -i lsblibchk-version.architecture.rpm
   ```

11.3.1.2 Running *lsblibchk*

You can run **lsblibchk** by executing the following command:

```
# /opt/lsb/bin/lsblibchk [-M modulename]
```

Example 11.4 shows the output of **lsblibchk**.

If there are any problems with the libraries, error messages will be displayed under the appropriate library symbol checking message. If your runtime environment contains more than one version of a library required by the specification, you should also verify that the correct library is located by the test program.

A file named journal.lsbchk (Example 11.5) is produced that contains detailed information on the tests performed and the results of those tests.

Example 11.4: Running **lsblibchk**

```
Checking symbols in /lib/ld-lsb.so.1
Checking symbols in /usr/lib/libGL.so.1
Checking symbols in /usr/X11R6/lib/libICE.so.6
Checking symbols in /usr/X11R6/lib/libSM.so.6
Checking symbols in /usr/X11R6/lib/libX11.so.6
Checking symbols in /usr/X11R6/lib/libXext.so.6
Checking symbols in /usr/X11R6/lib/libXt.so.6
Checking symbols in /lib/libc.so.6
Checking symbols in /lib/libcrypt.so.1
Checking symbols in /lib/libdl.so.2
Checking symbols in /lib/libm.so.6
Checking symbols in /lib/libncurses.so.5
Checking symbols in /lib/libpthread.so.0
Checking symbols in /lib/librt.so.1
Checking symbols in /lib/libutil.so.1
Checking symbols in /usr/lib/libz.so.1
```

Example 11.5: A `journal.lsbchk` File

```
0|lsb-0.1 14:50:07 20040113\
|User: nicole (0) TCC Start, Command line: libchk
5|Linux suefan.chelsea.com 2.4.20-8 \
#1 Sat Aug 26 13:24:28 EST 1984 i686\
|System Information
30||VSX_NAME=lsblibchk version
10|1 /lib/ld-lsb.so.1 14:50:07|
400|1 1 14:50:07|IC Start
200|1 1 14:50:07|Looking for library /lib/ld-lsb.so.1
220|1 1 0 14:50:07|PASS
520|1 1 0 0 0|FILE_SIZE 104560
520|1 1 0 0 0|BINARY_MD5SUM=f727976f21ce43e021a77c8bd96e82db
410|1 1 14:50:07|IC End
400|1 2 14:50:07|IC Start
200|1 2 14:50:07|Check header id EI_MAG0 is ELFMAG0
220|1 2 0 14:50:07|PASS
410|1 2 14:50:07|IC End
400|1 3 14:50:07|IC Start
200|1 3 14:50:07|Check header id EI_MAG1 is ELFMAG1
220|1 3 0 14:50:07|PASS
410|1 3 14:50:07|IC End
400|1 4 14:50:07|IC Start
200|1 4 14:50:07|Check header id EI_MAG2 is ELFMAG2
220|1 4 0 14:50:07|PASS
410|1 4 14:50:07|IC End
400|1 5 14:50:07|IC Start
```

```
200|1 5 14:50:07|Check header id EI_MAG3 is ELFMAG3
220|1 5 0 14:50:07|PASS
410|1 5 14:50:07|IC End
400|1 6 14:50:07|IC Start
200|1 6 14:50:07|Check header id EI_CLASS is ELFCLASS32
220|1 6 0 14:50:07|PASS
410|1 6 14:50:07|IC End
400|1 7 14:50:07|IC Start
200|1 7 14:50:07|Check header id EI_DATA is ELFDATA2LSB
220|1 7 0 14:50:07|PASS
410|1 7 14:50:07|IC End
400|1 8 14:50:07|IC Start
200|1 8 14:50:07|Check header id EI_VERSION is EV_CURRENT
220|1 8 0 14:50:07|PASS
410|1 8 14:50:07|IC End
400|1 9 14:50:07|IC Start
200|1 9 14:50:07|Check header id EI_OSABI is ELFOSABI_SYSV
220|1 9 0 14:50:07|PASS
410|1 9 14:50:07|IC End
400|1 10 14:50:07|IC Start
200|1 10 14:50:07|Check header id EI_ABIVERSION is 0
220|1 10 0 14:50:07|PASS
410|1 10 14:50:07|IC End
400|1 11 14:50:07|IC Start
200|1 11 14:50:07|Check header field e_type is ET_DYN
220|1 11 0 14:50:07|PASS
410|1 11 14:50:07|IC End
400|1 12 14:50:07|IC Start
200|1 12 14:50:07|Check header field e_machine is EM_386
220|1 12 0 14:50:07|PASS
410|1 12 14:50:07|IC End
400|1 13 14:50:07|IC Start
200|1 13 14:50:07|Check header field e_version is EV_CURRENT
220|1 13 0 14:50:07|PASS
410|1 13 14:50:07|IC End
400|1 14 14:50:07|IC Start
200|1 14 14:50:07|Check header field e_flags is 0
220|1 14 0 14:50:07|PASS
410|1 14 14:50:07|IC End
10|2 libc.so.6 14:50:07|
400|2 1 14:50:07|IC Start
200|2 1 14:50:07|Looking for library libc.so.6
520|2 1 0 0 0|Found match for libc.so.6 as /lib/tls/libc.so.6
```

11.3.2   Using `lsb-test-pam`

The `lsb-test-pam` test verifies the mechanics of authentication from the applications and enables the local system administrator to choose how individual applications will authenticate users.

11.3.2.1   Installing `lsb-test-pam`

Complete the following steps to install `lsb-test-pam`:

1. Download the package from the LSB Download Web site.[7]

2. Install the binary RPM package using the following command:

   ```
   # rpm -ihv  lsb-test-pam-version.architecture.rpm
   ```

11.3.2.2   Running `lsb-test-pam`

1. Log out and log in as the user vsx0. You may need to first set the password for this account as it is not set to anything during the installation of the package.

2. Execute `run_tests` using the following command:

   ```
   vsx0$ ./run_tests
   ```

   Example 11.6 shows how to run `lsb-test-pam`.

Example 11.6: Running `lsb-test-pam`

```
Name of person running tests (Automated)? Sparky
Organization (NONE)?  TSMA
Test System (UNKNOWN)?  lsbtest1
Block special filename ()?
Enter name of the user for PAM tests [vsx0] :
Enter password of the user for PAM tests : ******
Enter password of the test user vsx1 : ******
Enter password of the test user vsx2 : ******
Install /etc/pam.d/lsbpam_conf ..? [y]
Enter root password: ******
Password:
Updating the account properties of users vsx1 and vsx2
      sets the vsx1 account to have a password that needs to be updated
      sets the vsx2 account to be expired
Enter root password: ******
Password:
```

Example 11.7 shows a journal file for `lsb-test-pam`.

---

7. http://www.linuxbase.org/download/

Example 11.7: A Journal File for `lsb-test-pam`

```
tcc: journal file is /home/tet/test_sets/results/0001e/journal
09:57:36 Execute /tset/LSB.pam/testcases/pam_authenticate/pam_authenticate
09:57:42 Execute /tset/LSB.pam/testcases/pam_acct_mgmt/pam_acct_mgmt
09:57:43 Execute /tset/LSB.pam/testcases/pam_close_session/pam_close_session
09:57:44 Execute /tset/LSB.pam/testcases/pam_getenvlist/pam_getenvlist
09:57:45 Execute /tset/LSB.pam/testcases/pam_get_item/pam_get_item
09:57:46 Execute /tset/LSB.pam/testcases/pam_open_session/pam_open_session
09:57:47 Execute /tset/LSB.pam/testcases/pam_set_item/pam_set_item
09:57:48 Execute /tset/LSB.pam/testcases/pam_start/pam_start
09:57:49 Execute /tset/LSB.pam/testcases/pam_end/pam_end
09:57:50 Execute /tset/LSB.pam/testcases/pam_fail_delay/pam_fail_delay
09:58:19 Execute /tset/LSB.pam/testcases/pam_chauthtok/pam_chauthtok
09:58:29 Execute /tset/LSB.pam/testcases/pam_setcred/pam_setcred
09:58:30 Execute /tset/LSB.pam/testcases/pam_strerror/pam_strerror

Results:
Total tests:   46 PASS = 46 FAIL = 0

Pass Breakdown:

Number of successes:    44 Number of warnings:      0
Number unsupported:     0 Number not in use:      2
Number of untested:     0 Number of FIP:        0
Unapproved assertions:  0 Number not implemented: 0

Failure Breakdown:
Number of failures:   0 Number unresolved:   0
Number uninitiated:   0 Number unreported:   0

Producing formal report (/home/tet/test_sets/results/report.200403260903)

Finished.
```

11.4   EXPANDING THE LSB TEST SUITES

This section describes how to expand the test suite by adding new tests.

11.4.1   Criteria for New Test Suites

For test cases to be useful for certification testing, they should meet several of the following criteria:

The Test Specification

- The premise for all the tests is that they have to be based on a written, publicly available test specification.

- The test specification upon which the test suite is based shall conform to the POSIX.3 methodology (which means the use of test assertions).

The Test Suite

- The test suite must be aligned with the current draft or issue of the relevant specification (mandatory).

- The test suite must be able to establish conformance with all legitimate options and variables defined by the specification (mandatory).

- Each individually executable test must provide its own setup and cleanup functionality (mandatory).

- No individually executable test shall introduce side effects that may affect the results of any other tests (mandatory).

- The unit of test execution should cover no more than a single interface function (desirable).

- The test suite shall have a capability to check complete and correct configuration and installation; this may include a set of defined confidence checks (mandatory).

- Configuration and installation checking facilities should be automated (desirable).

- The test suite must include clear and comprehensive user and programmer documentation.

 These criteria are taken from the Open Group's test suite acceptance criteria.[8]

---

8. http://www.opengroup.org/openbrand/testing/testprocs/accprocs.html

11.4.2   Writing TET-Based Test Suites

This section will help you understand the test development process at a high level. This process includes the following high level steps.

11.4.2.1   Developing the Specification

The specification should include the following information about the test suite:

- Test methodology
- Functional coverage
- Test architecture
- Assumptions
- Development schedule

11.4.2.2   Developing the Set of Formal Assertions

The purpose of this step is to create a list of testable statements from the specification. This is an intermediate step between the language of the specification and actual test code.

Formal test assertions should bridge the gap between the language of the specification and the test suite code. Likewise, the goal of the test code is to produce an executable representation of the requirements of the specification. Test suites developed with the assertion-based technique should meet the following requirements:

- They must follow the IEEE Standard for test methods (1003.3).
- An assertion must be developed for each definitive statement in the specification under the test.
- Each assertion must be designed to test whether the statement is true or false for the implementation under test.

11.4.2.3   Review of Assertions

The review of assertions helps to identify bad assumptions made by the writer of the assertions as well as ambiguities or errors in the specification being tested.

11.4.2.4   Test Case Development

This involves mapping the assertions to actual code that attempts to verify them. Test case writers should attempt to follow the guidelines listed in Section 11.4.1, in particular, only test one thing at a time and avoid having side effects between test cases. These two properties are especially valuable when attempting to debug test failures.

11.4.2.5   Test Case Review

Having the test cases run by other people on a wide variety of implementations helps pick up problems in test case code and the underlying specification. Test case reviews are used to validate the test suite. Reviews should conform to the following guidelines:

- Use review guidelines and pro-forma responses.
- Comments should be specific.
- Comments should include a specific action.

11.4.3   Converting Existing Test Suites to Use the TET/VSXgen Framework

There are two methods of converting existing test cases to be usable in the TET/VSXgen framework used by the LSB. This section describes each method.

11.4.3.1   Adding the TET-Specific Calls to the Original Test Case Source Code

This method is best suited for test cases that include a series of macros. For example:

```
ASSERT(foo==5, "Foo was not 5");
```

The macro can be changed to the appropriate TET calls making the test suite TET-aware without a lot of intrusive code changes. If changes are not possible, it is still possible to manually add the TET calls.

11.4.3.2   *Wrapping the Binaries in TET-Aware Shell Code*

This method is best suited for test cases that return with informative exit codes or output parseable error messages, so that a shell script wrapper can be used to convert these to TET return codes. While this method allows for the reuse of existing test case code, it might make test suites harder to debug and results harder to understand.

11.5   DOWNLOADING THE LSB TEST SUITES

To obtain LSB Test Suites go to LSB Download Web page.[9] Table 11.1 represents the information that can be accessed via the World Wide Web.

Table 11.1: Test Suite Download Page

Specification Version	*Package*	*Version*	*Architecture*
2.0	`lsb-runtime-test`	2.0.0–1	I486, IA64, PPC, PPC64, S390, S390X, x86_64, SRC
2.0	`lsb-test-pam`	2.0.0–1	I486, IA64, PPC, PPC64, S390, S390X, x86_64, SRC
2.0	`lsb-test-vsw4`	2.0.0–1	I486, IA64, PPC, PPC64, S390, S390X, x86_64, SRC
2.0	`lsb-test-c++`	2.0.0–1	I486, IA64, PPC, PPC64, S390, S390X, x86_64, SRC
2.0	`lsblibchk`	2.0.0–1	I486, IA64, PPC, PPC64, S390, S390X, x86_64, SRC

---

9. `http://www.linuxbase.org/download/`

`lsb-runtime-test`   This is a binary version of the LSB Runtime test suites.

`lsb-test-pam`   This is a binary version of the LSB PAM test suites.

`lsb-test-vsw4`   This is a binary version of the LSB X Window System test suite. These tests are derived from the VSW4 XTest test suites.

`lsb-test-c++`   This is a binary version of the LSB C++ test suite.

`lsblibchk`   This is a program that looks for LSB libraries and checks that those libraries contain the symbols required by the specification. If it is required that the symbol be versioned, this program checks that the symbol with the correct version exists in the library, and can be used for checking either the LSB Runtime Environment or the LSB Development Environment.

## CHAPTER TWELVE

Using the Sample Implementation

The LSB Sample Implementation (LSB-si) is a minimal LSB-conformant runtime environment used for testing purposes. Think of it as a tiny Linux distribution that you have complete control over. It can be booted as a standalone system, hosted inside a virtual machine, or run in a change-root mode. It is particularly convenient to use hosted mode as a way to enable an LSB test environment to exist on a system without disrupting the base system, thus reducing the need for multiple dedicated LSB test machines.

LSB-compliant applications should be tested inside the LSB-si to insure they haven't picked up any distribution-specific quirks. The LSB Certification program, as outlined in Chapter 7, requires that an application be tested under the LSB-si.

The LSB-si can also be used in a variety of validation scenarios where there's a desire to limit the installed environment to the minimal set required by the LSB.

12.1 UNDERSTANDING THE SAMPLE IMPLEMENTATION

The LSB-si is an example runtime environment implementation. It is the accumulation of elements that are both explicitly required and implied by the LSB Written Specification, plus any necessary dependencies to make the runtime environment work.

The LSB-si has three main purposes. First, it is an example implementation to demonstrate the features and correctness of the LSB Written Specification. Second, it serves as an example of building an LSB-conformant system from current open source packages without a lot of special patching. Thirdly, the LSB-si is a testing sandbox to help evaluate the LSB compliance of an application. If an application fails because it requires something not found in the LSB-si, then this is an opportunity to trim or rework the dependencies of an application to help better conform to the LSB.

The LSB-si is a *sample implementation*, not a *reference implementation*. The difference is that a sample implementation demonstrates one way to conform to the specification, while a reference implementation serves as a baseline for conformance validation. In a reference implementation scenario, other implementors are required to be compatible with all of the reference implementation, including all the features and bugs unintentially present in it. In addition, a reference implementation constrains the evolution of other implementations because even legitimate enhancements or fixes would deviate from the reference, thus breaking adherence.

The LSB is an ABI specification designed to capture the functional requirements of a conforming system without locking in any specific implementation, versions of software packages, and so on, as being the standard. By specifying the behavior of required elements and avoiding a reference implementation, the LSB permits conforming runtime environments and applications to evolve within the ABI confines of the Written Specification.

12.2   SETTING UP THE SAMPLE IMPLEMENTATION

The LSB-si can be run in one of three different modes: the `chroot` LSB-si, the UML LSB-si, and the bootable Knoppix LSB-si. Software for each mode can be downloaded from the LSB Download Web site.[1]

---

1. `http://www.linuxbase.org/download/`

12.2.1   Sample Implementation Using `chroot(1)`

The `chroot` LSB-si is distributed as a compressed tarball that should simply be unpacked by the superuser (Example 12.1). Later, other pieces can be layered on top of it, and packages for additional functionality can be installed inside it. For illustrative purposes, the IA32 (x86) architecture will be used in the following examples. For your situation, you may need to substitute the appropriate LSB architecture and version.

Example 12.1: Installing LSB-si on IA32 (x86) Architecture

```
# mkdir /opt/lsbsi-ia32
# cd /opt
# tar jxvf /tmp/lsbsi-ia32-2.0.1.tar.bz2
```

The LSB-si can be started by running the `/sbin/chroot` command (Example 12.2; some distributions place this command in `/usr/sbin`).

Example 12.2: Starting LSB-si by the `/sbin/chroot` Command

```
# /sbin/chroot /opt/lsbsi-ia32
```

To simulate a login session, use this command as shown in Example 12.3.

Example 12.3: Login Session

```
# /sbin/chroot /opt/lsbsi-ia32 /bin/bash -l
```

When working in the `chroot`, only files inside the `chroot` tree will be accessible. Since this limits the usefulness of the environment, some steps should be taken ahead of time to make the necessary files available. One approach is to simply copy files from the `chroot` into a suitable location. If another window or terminal session is available on the host system, it is also possible to copy files into the `chroot` tree the same way, whenever they are needed (Example 12.4).

Example 12.4: Copying Files into `chroot`

```
# cp mypackage.rpm /opt/lsbsi-ia32/tmp
```

Another approach is to establish bind mounts before starting the `chroot`. These bind mounts enable portions of the filesystem of the host to appear to be inside of the `chroot`. Bind-mounting a user's home directory to the same location in the `chroot` will make that user's files appear in the same path inside the `chroot` as on the host system. Example 12.5 shows setting up access to the files in the home directory of `username`.

Example 12.5: Bind Mounts

```
# mkdir /opt/lsbsi-ia32/home/username
# mount -o bind /home/username /opt/lsbsi-ia32/home/username
```

 This does not cause the user account itself to exist in the `chroot`. The **useradd** command should be used to add the account. The account should be given the same `userid` as it has on the host system.

The LSB-si limits itself to commands and features required by the LSB Written Specification, which is a set chosen to be able to minimally install, configure, and administer installed software. This has some testing benefits, but this also means there likely are a few missed components. These are not hard to work around, but the LSB-si philosophy leaves them out; by having to install them specifically, you become aware of these areas that are actually not standard across systems.

The **rpm** tool needs access to /proc to calculate disk space (the mounted filesystem table is found through /proc). However, /proc is not part of the LSB Written Specification. The simplest workaround is to add a line describing it to the /etc/fstab of the LSB-si so that you can simply say `mount /proc`. Example 12.6 shows such a line, through it is best to simply copy the line from /etc/fstab on the host system.

Example 12.6: Adding /proc to `fstab`

```
none   /proc   proc   defaults   0 0
```

Depending on your requirements, you may also need to perform similar steps for other pseudo filesystems such as /dev/shm and /dev/pts.

Some of the commands you may be accustomed to may be missing, including editors and development tools. Many developers have found it useful to work in a windowed environment, with one window running the LSB-si chroot and others set up to be able to edit and otherwise modify files as necessary.

Example 12.7 illustrates copying an installable package into the chroot tree, starting the chroot, installing the package, and running it. As this example will utilize the X Server on the host system, an additional setup step to enable access to this server is included before the chroot is started.

Example 12.7: Installing a Package on chroot

```
# cp lsb-xpaint-2.6.2-3.i486.rpm /opt/lsbsi-ia32/tmp
# xhost +localhost

# /sbin/chroot /opt/lsbsi-ia32
# cd /tmp
# rpm -i lsb-xpaint-2.6.2-3.i486.rpm
# rpm -qa
# export DISPLAY=localhost:0
# /opt/lsb-xpaint/bin/xpaint
```

For networked applications, some additional support is probably needed. For example, the /etc/services file is not described by the LSB, and thus is not present in the chroot. If needed, simply copy it over from the host system.

Also, if a server (daemon) is to be tested, it will first need to be set up to listen on the appropriate port; secondly, any conflicting service on the host system must be disabled so the connection actually reaches the daemon in the LSB-si `chroot`.

The base LSB-si does not have the **inetd** or **xinetd** servers, so by default these cannot be used to listen for service requests. The `lsbsi-archtest` package can be installed to provide **inetd**. Example 12.8 shows a normal run of `lsb-runtime-test` to validate the LSB-si. The `lsb-test` package is previously installed. One part of testing requires the **syslog** daemon, so the `syslogd` from the host system is shut down first. The test setup requires a true login, so **inetd** is started to watch over a **telnet** daemon.

Example 12.8: Using the `lsb-test` Package to Run **inetd**

```
# sh /etc/init.d/syslog stop
# /usr/sbin/chroot /opt/lsbsi-ia32
# mount /proc
# /sbin/syslogd -m 0
# /usr/sbin/inetd
```

Now connect to the LSB-si `chroot` using telnet, and log in as a user defined inside the LSB-si (Example 12.9).

Example 12.9: Connecting to `chroot`

```
$ telnet localhost
```

12.2.2   Sample Implementation Using UML

The UML LSB-si runs off a *root filesystem* that is encapsulated in a file. The LSB-si will not be able to "see" outside this filesystem except if running `hostfs`, in which case the filesystem tree of the host can be mounted and accessed. This is the easiest way to get files, such as packages, to be installed into the UML LSB-si.

It is also possible to copy files into the `root_fs` (root filesystem file) of the UML LSB-si. This is a little tricky, so proceed carefully (Example 12.10).

Example 12.10: Copy Files into `root_fs`

```
# mkdir /mnt/lsbsi
# losetup /dev/loop0 /opt/lsb-umlsi/lib/root_fs
# mount /dev/loop0 /mnt/lsbsi
# cp lsb-lynx-2.8.4-1.i486.rpm /mnt/lsbsi/tmp
# umount /mnt/lsbsi
# losetup -d /dev/loop0
```

The UML LSB-si is started by running the User-Mode Linux kernel; a script is provided by the installable (RPM or Debian) packages to do this with appropriate arguments. If it has not been run previously, the `Configure` script will be run now to set up important parts of the hosted UML Sample Implementation (Example 12.11).

Example 12.11: Running the `Configure` Script

```
# /opt/lsb-umlsi/bin/umlsi
```

An advantage of using the UML is that it allows the whole system, kernel and all, to be run in user space. This enables the testing and debugging of an LSB-supporting kernel without actually installing a new kernel on the host system. In addition, UML more stringently isolates the LSB-si from the hosting system.

12.2.3   Using a Bootable Sample Implementation

The base tarball plus the `lsbsi-arch-boot` tarball are nearly enough for a complete standalone bootable system. The two missing pieces are a Linux kernel and a bootloader setup, plus some final configuration needs to be done manually. Examples 12.12 to 12.15 show the steps to build a bootable LSB-si partition on an already-bootable system. You will need to augment further to put these on a "fresh" system with no existing Linux installation.

Locate an unused partition, such as `/dev/sda9`, and make an appropriate filesystem on it (the `-j` option to **mke2fs** is used to create a journaling (ext3) filesystem). This partition will now contain most of a runnable system. There are a few more things that need to be done to it, such as building the correct filesystem mount table and setting up a kernel that works appropriately for this system.

Example 12.12: Creating a Journaling Filesystem

```
# mke2fs -j /dev/sda9
# mkdir /mnt/lsbsi
# mount empty-partition /mnt/lsbsi
# cd /mnt
# tar -xvjf /tmp/lsbsi-ia32-2.0.0.tar.bz2
# cd lsbsi
# tar -xvjf /tmp/lsbsi-test-ia32-2.0.0.tar.bz2
```

1. Handcraft an appropriate /etc/fstab that describes the root filesystem, swap (if any), and any additional mounts, including special filesystems such as /proc, /dev/pts, and so on.

2. Copy over the modules directory matching a bootable kernel that already works on this system (Example 12.13).

Example 12.13: Copying the modules Directory

```
# cp -r /lib/modules/2.4.18-24.8.0 /mnt/lsbsi/lib/modules
# cp /boot/vmlinuz-2.4.18-24.8.0 /mnt/lsbsi/boot
```

3. Copy over a working /etc/modules.conf or similar, as appropriate for the system you will be running (Example 12.14).

Example 12.14: Copying /etc/modules.conf

```
# cp /etc/modules.conf /mnt/lsbsi/etc
```

4. Add instructions to boot the kernel of your choice using the appropriate partition to boot to. For example, to boot using **lilo**, you might add the contents of Example 12.15 to /etc/lilo.conf.

Example 12.15: `/etc/lilo.conf` Instructions to Boot to **lilo**

```
image=/boot/vmlinuz-2.4.18-24.8.0
        label=lsbsi-boot
        root=/dev/sda9
        initrd=/boot/initrd-2.4.18-24.8.0.img
        read-only
```

If you're using a bootloader such as **lilo** that requires running a command to install the new configuration, don't forget to do so!

12.2.4 Sample Implementation Using Knoppix

Knoppix[2] is a bootable CD that runs GNU/Linux in memory without disturbing the operating system installed on the hard disk. The LSB has a version of Knoppix with the LSB-si configured on it. This disk is useful for demonstrating the LSB-si or for a tutorial lab use. When used for a demo or in a tutorial lab, there should be no concerns about what kernel, compiler, or **glibc** libraries are installed. Almost everyone can simply insert the disk into their computer and reboot to run Knoppix LSB-si.

12.3 APPLICATION TESTING USING THE SAMPLE IMPLEMENTATION

The LSB-si is equipped with a copy of **rpm**, to meet the requirement that a conformant platform be able to install RPM packages of the specified format. Note that **rpm** itself is not required by the LSB Written Specification. The RPM database in the LSB-si is populated with a minimal set of `provides`. As required by the specification, it provides a versioned **lsb** package dependency that matches the LSB Written Specification version, that is, `lsb=1.3` for LSB version 1.3, and `lsb=2.0` for LSB version 2.0. The LSB Written Specification permits, but does not require, an implementation of a later version to also support an earlier version, but the LSB-si does not attempt multiple-version compatibility.

---

2. `http://www.knopper.net/`

The LSB project has developed a package verification tool **lsbpkgchk** that should be run and whose output should be examined carefully. As of this writing, there were still some false negatives—warnings or errors that would not prevent a package from installing correctly (it appears that there is no version of **rpm** that 100% follows the rules in the LSB Written Specification). See the **lsbpkgchk** release notes for more information.

Packages need to be installed with normal dependency checking. Do not resort to installing with `rpm --nodeps`, as one of the purposes of testing in the LSB-si is to show that a given package can properly be installed by a strictly conforming implementation, and bending the rules by bypassing the dependency checking of **rpm** weakens this test.

Please report any issues back to the LSB team, preferably by filing a bug in the LSB Bugzilla[3] bugtracker.

Example 12.16 shows the installation of an **rpm** package. The package should now be ready to test in the normal way.

Example 12.16: Dependency Checking

```
# rpm -i /tmp/lsb-lynx-2.8.4-1.i486.rpm
```

12.4   BUILDING THE SAMPLE IMPLEMENTATION

It is not necessary to compile the LSB-si for testing; the official packages released by the LSB project should be used for this purpose. However, it may be instructive to see how the LSB-si is constructed to get to a clean implementation of the LSB Written Specification. The remainder of this section describes the process.

The LSB-si is built from clean upstream package sources. The build instructions are captured in a set of XML files that serve as input to a tool called **nALFS**; the concept is derived from the Linux From Scratch[4] project.

---

3. http://bugs.linuxbase.org

4. http://www.linuxfromscratch.org

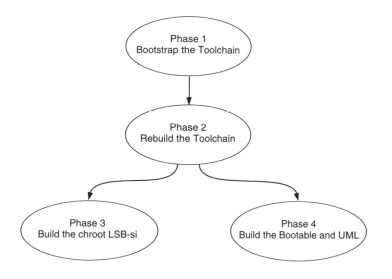

Figure 12.1: LSB-si Build

The build is a multistage process (Figure 12.1), so that the final result has been built by the LSB-si itself, and the majority of dependencies on the build environment of the host machine are eliminated. Ideally, all the dependencies would be eliminated, but in practice a few minor things may leak through. In particular, the initial stage of the LSB-si build now does not do the GCC fixincludes step as this pulled in some details of the host system in the "fixed" header files that were then used throughout the build process.

The **first phase**, or bootstrap, of the LSB-si build is to produce a minimal toolchain of static binaries as shown in Figure 12.1. Packages such as gcc, binutils, kernel-headers, and coreutils are built.

The **second phase** of the build is to use the bootstrap as a chroot environment to build a more complete toolchain as shown in Figure 12.1. As binaries are rebuilt, the new ones are installed on top of the old static copies built in the bootstrap phase so that by the end of the second phase, we have a complete development environment, using all dynamic libraries. This environment has the characteristic that it is entirely isolated from the details of the build host environment, since none of the tools from the build host have been used to compile the final binaries and libraries.

To reduce the rebuild time, the bootstrap phase is copied to another location before starting, and the copy is used as phase 2. During LSB-si development, there tend to be few changes to the bootstrap, but many to the later phases. For a released LSB-si source tree, this really doesn't matter except that it increases the space requirements of the build area a bit. Thus the bootstrap copy of second phase is not essential for the build strategy, but rather a convenience for LSB-si developers.

This intermediate phase 2 of the build can be used as an LSB Development Environment; in effect, this is what it does when building the final phase. The final phase does not have a compilation environment, as that is not part of the LSB Written Specification. The intermediate phase 2 is designed to be used as a `chroot` environment; using the compiler directly (not in a `chroot`) won't work as things will point relatively to the wrong places. Although the intermediate phase 2 is for the same architecture as the host machine, it is more like a cross-compilation environment. Note that producing a more usable build environment is a future direction; the current intermediate phase is not officially supported as such and the bundle is not part of the released materials.

The **third phase** is the construction of the actual LSB-si as it will be delivered as shown in Figure 12.1. In this phase, the completed second phase is used in a `chroot` as the development environment, and each package is then compiled and installed to a target location in the LSB-si tree. During the third phase, care is taken not to install unnecessary binaries or libraries, because an upstream source package will often build and install more than is required by the LSB, and these need to be pruned from the final tree.

Since the LSB team has already anticipated several uses for the LSB-si that require more than the core set, there exists a **fourth phase** that builds add-on bundles that can be installed on top of the base LSB-si bundle to provide additional functionality as shown in Figure 12.1. There are currently three subphases of the fourth phase: the first one to build additional tools required for running the `lsb-runtime-test` suite on the LSB-si, the second to build additional binaries to make a bootable system, and the third to build additional binaries to make a User-Mode Linux system. The fourth phase is built by the second phase build environment just like third phase is, and is completely independent of the third phase. That is, if one had a completed second phase, one could start off a fourth phase build without ever building the third phase and it would work fine. It is likely that in the future, there will be additional fourth phase subphases to include in a build environment.

12.4.1   Sample Implementation Build Process

The source code for the LSB-si Development Environment can be obtained from the LSB CVS tree. The code can be checked out in several ways: as a snapshot either by release tag or by date, or as a working cvs directory (even if you're not an LSB developer, having a working directory can let you check developments more quickly by doing a "cvs update"). For an example using a release-tag snapshot, see the build instructions in Section 12.4.2.

You can browse the CVS tree Web interface to determine the available release tags.

You will also need to check out (or export) the `tools/nALFS` directory to get the build tool. Again, see Section 12.4.2 for an example.

Source code for the patches to the base tarballs is in the CVS tree in `si/build/patches`. These patches should be copied to the package source directory. The base tarballs must be obtained separately. Once the build area has been configured, a provided tool can be used to populate the package source directory.

The same tool (`extras/entitycheck.py`) can be used to check if all the necessary files are present before starting a build. With a `-c` option, it will do a more rigorous test, checking md5sums, not just existence. Every effort has been made to describe reliable locations for the files, but sometimes a project chooses to move an old version aside after releasing a new one (if they have a history of doing so, the location where old versions are placed is probably already captured). The packages are also mirrored on the Free Standards Group Web site.[5] Still, retrieval sometimes fails; `entitycheck.py` will inform of missing files and the expected locations are listed in `extras/package_locations` so it's possible to try to fetch the missing packages manually.

---

5. `http://ftp.freestandards.org/pub/lsb/impl/`

12.4.2   Sample Implementation Build Steps

1. Obtain LSB-si sources from CVS:

```
$ export CVSROOT
$ CVSROOT=":pserver:anonymous@cvs.gforge.freestandards.org:\
/cvsroot/lsb"
$ cvs -d $CVSROOT export -r lsbsi-2.0_1 si/build
```

   Use -D now instead of the release tag to grab the current development version.

2. Configure the build environment. There's a simple configuration script that localizes the makefile, some of the entities, and other bits. The main question is where you're going to build the LSB-si. The default location is /usr/src/si. Make sure the build directory exists and is in a place that has enough space (see the note at the end of this section).

```
$ cd src/si
$ ./Configure
```

   Answer the questions.

3. From here on, you'll need to operate as superuser, as the build process does mounts and the chroot command, operations restricted to root in most environments.

4. Copy patches to their final destination (substitute your build directory if not using the default):

```
# cp patches/* /usr/src/si/packages
```

5. Check that the package and patch area is up to date:

```
# python extras/entitycheck.py -f
```

6. You're now ready to build the LSB-si:

```
# make
```

7. If there's a problem, **make** should restart the build where it failed. If the interruption happened during the intermediate LSB-si phase, it is likely that the whole phase will be restarted; this is normal.

8. Building the add-on packages `lsbsi-test`, `lsbsi-boot`, and `lsbsi-uml` requires an additional step. This step is not dependent on the LSB-si (phase 3) step having completed, but it is dependent on the intermediate LSB-si (phase 2) step being complete:

```
# make addons
```

9. Now you can build the UML installable package (IA-32 build host or target only). This step is dependent on all of the other phases, including the add-ons, having completed:

```
# cd rpm
# make
```

 The build takes a lot of space (around 1.4GB), and may take a lot of time. A full build on a fast dual-CPU Pentium 4 is about 2.5 hours; depending on architecture, memory, and processor speed it may take as much as 20 hours.

If the build stops, voluntarily or through some problem, there should be a fair bit of support for restartability, but this is not perfect. In particular, be cautious about cleaning out any of the build areas, as the package directory may still be bind-mounted. Each of the team members has accidentally removed the packages directory more than once, causing big delays while it's being refetched (it pays to make a copy of this directory somewhere else). Be careful! The makefile has a `clear_mounts` target that may be helpful.

12.5 TESTING THE SAMPLE IMPLEMENTATION

The LSB-si (Figure 12.2) is subjected to the same testing regiment as described in Chapter 6:

1. `lsb-runtime-test`, with objective being zero failures

2. `lsblibchk`, to check that all the required libraries are present

3. Application Battery, running the FVTs for all the example applications

Install the LSB Runtime tests into the LSB-si `chroot` environment (Example 12.17).

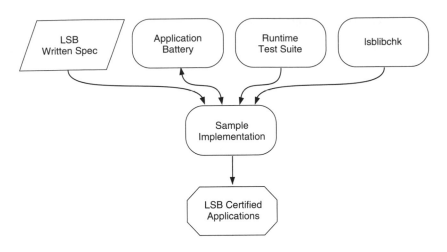

Figure 12.2: Sample Implementation

Example 12.17: Runtime Test Installation

```
# cp lsb-runtime-test-2.0-1.ia32.rpm /opt/lsbsi-ia32/tmp
# /sbin/chroot /opt/lsbsi-ia32
# cd /tmp
# rpm -i lsb-runtime-test-2.0-1.ia32.rpm
# password -d vsx0
```

As shown in Section 12.2.1, log in as user vsx0, then run the LSB Runtime test suite (Example 12.18).

Example 12.18: Running the Runtime Test Suite

```
vsx0$ telnet localhost
vsx0$ run_tests
```

12.6   PACKAGING THE SAMPLE IMPLEMENTATION

The LSB-si is released in several configurations for each of the following architectures:

1. **Base system**   A tarball containing only what is required by the LSB Written Specification. Can be entered via `chroot`. For complete conformance, requires the underlying Linux kernel to be LSB-conformant.

2. **Testable system**   Contains the base system plus additional files and programs needed to enable the LSB-si as a testing environment. This bundle can run the LSB Runtime test suite and LSB-conformant applications. Can be entered via `chroot`. Once running, it is possible to telnet into the environment. Complete conformance requires the underlying Linux kernel to be LSB-conformant.

3. **Bootable system**   The files from the base system plus a kernel and other support to make it possible to boot a standalone. Some additional configuration will be necessary—for example, an appropriate boot configuration for the target hardware and configuration of necessary kernel modules.

4. **Hosted system**   The files from the base system plus support to run User-Mode Linux, a kernel virtual machine that runs as a user-level application on the host system. User-Mode Linux may not be available for all LSB-supported architectures. The hosted bundle is also available as an installable, ready-to-run package.

 When the package is being extended beyond the base, there's a tradeoff: The system becomes more usable, but includes various non-LSB commands and files, and therefore is a little less "pure" in a testing sense.

12.7   Downloading the Sample Implementation

To download the LSB Sample Implementation go to the LSB Download Web site.[6] Table 12.1 represents the information that can be accessed via the World Wide Web.

lsbsi-boot   LSB Sample Implementation bootable system containing a kernel and other support to make it possible to boot the LSB-si in a standalone mode. Requires installation of lsbsi-core and post installation configuration.

lsbsi-core   LSB Sample Implementation base system containing only what is required by the LSB Written Specification. Can be entered via chroot.

lsbsi-graphics   LSB Sample Implementation graphics system containing the files necessary to support graphical applications within the LSB-si. Requires installation of lsbsi-core.

Table 12.1: Sample Implementation Download Page

Specification Version	Package	Version	Architecture
2.0.0	lsbsi-boot	2.0.2	IA32, IA64, PPC32, PPC64, S390, S390X, x86_64
2.0.0	lsbsi-core	2.0.2	IA32, IA64, PPC32, PPC64, S390, S390X, x86_64
2.0.0	lsb-graphics	2.0.2	IA32, IA64, PPC32, PPC64, S390, S390X, x86_64
2.0.0	lsb-test	2.0.2	IA32, IA64, PPC32, PPC64, S390, S390X, x86_64
2.0.0	lsb-uml	2.0.2	IA32, IA64, PPC32, PPC64, S390, S390X, x86_64

6. http://www.linuxbase.org/download/

lsbsi-test   LSB Sample Implementation testable system containing additional files and programs needed to enable the LSB-si as a testing environment. Requires installation of lsbsi-core.

lsbsi-uml   LSB Sample Implementation hosted system containing support to run User-Mode Linux, a kernel virtual machine that runs as a user-level application on the host system. UML may not be available for all LSB-supported architectures. Requires installation of lsbsi-core.

lsb   This package provides the base LSB package. Note that this package should only ever be installed on the LSB Sample Implementation. Installing this package on any other distribution may damage the system.

lsb-umlsi   LSB Sample Implementation User-Mode Linux environment.

## CHAPTER THIRTEEN

Using the LSB Development Environment

The LSB Development Environments are designed to help developers build applications which conform to the LSB Written Specification. They primarily do this by providing easy ways to

- Compile against header files that contain definitions required by the LSB Written Specification

- Dynamically link against shared libraries that contain only interfaces required by the LSB Written Specification

13.1 UNDERSTANDING THE LSB DEVELOPMENT ENVIRONMENT

The LSB Development Environment is not intended to be an Integrated Development Environment (IDE) in itself, but rather an enhancement to existing IDEs, to allow them to build binaries that are LSB-compliant. Note that although the LSB Development Environment helps programmers build LSB-compliant applications, it not the only way to do so.

13.2   GETTING THE LSB DEVELOPMENT ENVIRONMENT

The most recent information about the LSB Development Environments[1] can be found online. The packages for the Development Environment can be downloaded from the LSB Download Web site.[2]

13.3   USING THE LSB DEVELOPMENT ENVIRONMENT

There are three packages for the LSB Development Environments. The first is `lsb-build-base`, which contains the LSB-compliant header files and LSB shared stub libraries. The `lsb-build-cc` and `lsb-build-chroot` provide different methods for building an LSB-compliant binary. Both of these tools require the `lsb-build-base` package to also be installed.

13.3.1   LSB Shared Stub Libraries

The LSB Development Environment provides shared libraries that can be dynamically linked against an application. The functions within these libraries are stubs only (that is, they contain no executable code) and are not intended to be used, except for linking against when building a dynamically linked binary.

The environment in which software is developed is often different than that in which the application is designed to be run. For example, developers will often have a more recent version of the C library than what the LSB requires. Header files used during compilation can contain definitions that affect the runtime behavior of an application. For example, the content and size of structs can change as libraries develop, so it is important that the correct representation is used for the given version of the library.

In order to solve this problem, some libraries such as the C library use symbol versioning. Each interface within the library has a version associated with it, allowing for multiple versions of the same interface (such as `open`) to exist in the same shared library. The inclusion of multiple versions of a

---

1. http://www.linuxbase.org/build/

2. http://www.linuxbase.org/download/

function allows older applications to continue to use the old version, while new applications can use the new version.

When a binary is created, it inspects the shared library it is linking against and records the versions of those interfaces it requires. At runtime, the binary will look for the interfaces with the recorded version number, and fail if they do not exist. Thus, it is necessary to link against shared libraries that contain the versions of the interfaces guaranteed to exist on an LSB-compliant runtime.

Where libraries supported by the LSB use symbol versioning, the specification lists specific versions of the interfaces. The LSB stub libraries only contain the versions of the interfaces allowed by the LSB Written Specification, and so if they are used, it is impossible to use a wrong version when building a binary.

Often there are interfaces contained in shared libraries that must not be used by an LSB-compliant binary. These interfaces are often private functions, or interfaces not supported by the LSB. Since the stub libraries only contain interfaces required by the specification, an error will occur during the linking stage if an application uses an unsupported interface.

13.3.2 LSB Header Files

The definitions contained within a header file associated with a library may change over time as the ABI of that library evolves. For example, a function in one version of the library may take one parameter, while in the next version it may take two parameters.

The LSB Written Specification defines an ABI for each supported library, and the header files used to compile against that library must match exactly. In order to avoid the problem of finding the exact version of the software that contains the correct definitions, header files matching the specification are supplied with the LSB Development Environment.

13.3.3 Using the Development Tools

There are currently two development tools, `lsb-build-chroot` and `lsb-build-cc`, that compile and link against compliant headers and libraries.

Using these tools is an easy way to build an LSB-compliant application. Both tools use the `lsb-build-base` package. This package contains the LSB header files and stub libraries.

13.3.3.1   `lsb-build-chroot`

The `lsb-build-chroot` uses the **chroot** command to create a virtual LSB platform development environment on your machine. By default, it presents a minimal environment which, wherever possible, does not contain header files or libraries that, if compiled against, would lead to a binary that is not LSB-compliant. Within this environment, the `/usr/include` contains the LSB header files and the `/usr/lib` contains the LSB stub libraries.

To generate the virtual environment, the `lsb-build-chroot` uses bind mounts instead of copying the entire directory structure, so the disk space requirements are minimal. It also means that changes (such as compiling a binary) made within the environment are reflected immediately outside the environment, and vice versa.

You do not need root access to use `lsb-build-chroot` because it is implemented with an **ssh** daemon which is run on a high port. The **ssh** daemon bind-mounts your home directory into the `chroot` environment, so you can log in to the restricted environment for compilation. You can also run a full editing and debugging environment outside of the `chroot` operating on the same files that you are compiling within the restricted environment.

In cases where applications need to compile or link against libraries that are not LSB-compliant, you can specifically import those libraries and header files into the `chroot` environment. Depending on the sophistication of the build process for your application, you might also have to import other tools into the environment so that they can run correctly.

 The bind mounts might cause problems if you update system packages while `lsb-build-chroot` is running.

Simple example. In Example 13.1 we have a source file `hello_world.c`.

Example 13.1: `hello_world.c` Source File

```
#include <stdio.h>
#include <stdlib.h>

int main(int argc, char *argv[])
{
  printf("Hello World\n");
  exit(0);
}
```

First, we login into the restricted environment (Example 13.2). By default the **sshd** daemon for the environment listens on port 5436.

Example 13.2: Logging into the Restricted Environment

```
$ slogin -p 5436 localhost
lsbdevchroot$
```

We can then build the binary as we would normally (Example 13.3).

Example 13.3: Building and Running the Binary

```
lsbdevchroot$ gcc -Wall -o hello_world hello_world.c
lsbdevchroot$ ./hello_world
Hello World
lsbdevchroot$
```

Outside of the restricted environment, we could attach a debugger if we wish.

13.3.3.2 `lsb-build-cc`

The `lsb-build-cc` is a wrapper program for **gcc** that is invoked in place of the compiler. The wrapper program modifies the arguments passed to the actual compiler to ensure that your application uses the LSB-specified versions of header files and libraries instead of those installed on the system. However, the full functionality of the native system is available to build, develop, and debug the application. To use `lsb-build-cc`, you can use either of the commands shown in Example 13.4.

Example 13.4: `lsb-build-cc`

```
# CC=lsbcc ./configure
# CC=lsbc++ ./configure (for C++)
```

or

```
# CC=lsbcc make
# CC=lsbc++ make (for C++)
```

Further information about using **lsbcc** can be found in the man page included with the `lsb-build-cc` package.

Simple example.   In Example 13.5 we have a source file `hello_world.c`.

Example 13.5: `hello_world.c` Source File

```
#include <stdio.h>
#include <stdlib.h>

int main(int argc, char *argv[])
{
  printf("Hello World\n");
  exit(0);
}
```

Instead of calling **gcc** directly, we use **lsbcc** (Example 13.6).

Example 13.6: Using **lsbcc**

```
$ lsbcc -Wall -o hello_world hello_world.c
$ ./hello_world
Hello World
$
```

Hint.   Suppose `myfunction()` is an ABI provided by **libc** and it has different versions. If **myapplication** uses the `myfunction()` ABI, we could compare the application and the library images to see which ABI is actually used, as shown in Example 13.7.

Example 13.7: Testing **myapplication** against **glibc**

```
$ /usr/bin/objdump -T myapplication | grep myfunction
08048330 DF *UND* 00000032 GLIBC_2.0 myfunction

$ /usr/bin/objdump -T /lib/i686/libc.so.6 | egrep myfunction
000bb160 g DF .text 00000032 GLIBC_2.0 myfunction
000bb160 w DF .text 00000032 GLIBC_2.1 myfunction
```

The correct ABI for `myfunction()` used by **myapplication** should be `GLIBC_2.0` so that it will return a double. The library and the operating system are allowed to evolve, but the LSB refreshes less frequently to provide a stable runtime environment for applications.

13.3.3.3   Choosing

Table 13.1 explains when you should use `lsb-build-cc` and when you should use `lsb-build-chroot`.

Table 13.1: Using `lsb-build-cc` and `lsb-build-chroot`

Use `lsb-build-cc` *if:*	*Use* `lsb-build-chroot` *if:*
• Your application uses tools or shared libraries that are not available in `lsb-build-chroot`.	• Your application has hard-coded paths to include files and shared libraries.
• Your application has test scripts that are different from most Linux environments.	• Your application has hard-coded use of specific compilers in its makefile.
	• It is necessary to use a compiler other than GCC.

13.4   SHARED LIBRARIES

When an application uses a library that is not part of the LSB Written Specification, it can be built in one of two ways. Either the binary is statically linked against that library, or, if the library is LSB-compliant, it may be dynamically linked with the binary. If it is dynamically linked, the shared library must be supplied with the rest of the application.

The requirements for a shared library to be considered LSB-compliant are essentially the same as those required for a directly executable program. That is, it must only use dynamic interfaces supported by the specification, or alternatively supplied in another LSB-compliant shared library that is packaged with the rest of the application.

Much like an ordinary binary, a shared library that is to be supplied with an LSB-compliant application should be built against the LSB headers and stub libraries.

Do not build a shared library with **ld** (Example 13.8). This may lead to the use of symbol versions that are not part of the LSB Written Specification.

Example 13.8: Building a Library with **ld**

```
# ld -r -shared -o libtest.so obj1.o obj2.o
```

If you are using the `lsb-build-cc` technique of building an application, then shared libraries must also be built using **lsbcc** (Example 13.9).

Example 13.9: Building a Library with **lsbcc**

```
# gcc -shared -o libtest.so obj1.o obj2.o
```

If you are using the `lsb-build-chroot` technique for building an application, then no modifications to the build method are required.

When it comes to linking an application, if you use **lsbcc**, by default only the LSB-specified libraries will be linked dynamically, even if both static and shared libraries are available in the search path. This behavior can be modified by setting the environment variable LSBCC_SHAREDLIBS. Its value is a colon-separated list of library names that specifies which extra libraries should be dynamically linked.

If you use lsb-build-chroot then the compiler will dynamically link all shared libraries available in the restricted environment, and fall back to static linking if only the static version of a library is present.

13.5   CASE STUDY: RSYNC

The **rsync** application is one of the programs in the LSB Application Battery. We use this program as an example of the types of problems that developers may encounter, and how to work around them when attempting to build an LSB-compliant binary.

We use the **lsbcc** build tool with **rsync** version 2.5.5. The source for **rsync** can be downloaded from the **rsync** Web site.[3]

13.5.1   Building an rsync Binary with lsbcc

First, we unpack the sources and run the configure script (Example 13.10). We make sure that configure uses **lsbcc** as the compiler by setting the CC environment variable (and not cc, as configure might do otherwise by default).

From the edited configure output shown in Example 13.10, we can see that the configure script has correctly detected that mallinfo() is not part of the LSB, so it is not used. Although **libresolv** and **libpopt** are also not in the LSB Written Specification, **lsbcc** has detected that there is a static version of the library which can therefore be used.

Next, we attempt to compile the **rsync** binary (Example 13.11). Since we told the configure script to use **lsbcc** as the compiler, we do not need to set the CC environment variable when invoking **make**.

---

3. http://rsync.samba.org/

Example 13.10: Running the `configure` Script

```
$ tar xfz rsync-2.5.5.tar.gz
$ cd rsync-2.5.5/
$ CC=lsbcc ./configure
configure: Configuring rsync 2.5.5
checking build system type... i686-pc-linux-gnu
checking host system type... i686-pc-linux-gnu
checking target system type... i686-pc-linux-gnu
checking for gcc... lsbcc
checking for C compiler default output... a.out
checking whether the C compiler works... yes
...
checking for connect... yes
checking for inet_ntop in -lresolv... yes
checking for inet_ntop... yes
...
checking for mtrace... no
checking for mallinfo... no
checking for setgroups... yes
...
config.status: creating popt/dummy
config.status: creating shconfig
config.status: creating config.h

    rsync 2.5.5 configuration successful
```

Example 13.11: Compiling the **rsync** Binary

```
$ make
...
lsbcc -I. -I. -g -O2 -DHAVE_CONFIG_H -Wall -W -c clientname.c \
-o clientname.o
clientname.c: In function `client_sockaddr':
clientname.c:120: warning: implicit declaration of function \
`IN6_IS_ADDR_V4MAPPED'
clientname.c:120: dereferencing pointer to incomplete type
clientname.c:127: storage size of `sin6' isn't known
clientname.c:127: warning: unused variable `sin6'
clientname.c: In function `compare_addrinfo_sockaddr':
clientname.c:213: dereferencing pointer to incomplete type
```

An error has occurred during the compilation of `clientname.c`. Example 13.12 shows the code around line of 120 of `clientname.c`.

Example 13.12: The Source Context of the Compilation Error

```
...
#ifdef INET6
if (get_sockaddr_family(ss) == AF_INET6 &&
IN6_IS_ADDR_V4MAPPED(&((struct sockaddr_in6 *)ss)->sin6_addr)) {
/* OK, so ss is in the IPv6 family, but it is really
 * an IPv4 address: something like
...
```

We see here that the code is attempting to use IPv6 routines. LSB 1.3 did not support IPv6 and so the header files do not contain the macro definitions that this excerpt of code requires. Unfortunately, the `configure` script did not pick this problem up because it assumes that if a certain version (or better) of **glibc** is installed then the development system supports IPv6. It would be better to instead test directly that some IPv6 macros and interfaces exist.

Fortunately IPv6 support can be manually disabled by passing a parameter to the `configure` script. So we reconfigure and invoke **make** again (Example 13.13).

> LSB 2.0 and above has support for IPv6, so this workaround is not required.

Now, a link error has occurred—the linker was unable to find the `getpass()` function. The `getpass()` is not in the LSB Written Specification (the man page for it on Linux has it marked as obsolete), so a stub for it is not contained in the LSB C stub library. The info page for **glibc** suggests an alternative method, so we patch the **rsync** source code with suggested code excerpt. After that, the **make** succeeds and produces an **rsync** binary.

Example 13.13: Running `configure` without IPv6

```
$ ./configure --disable-ipv6
configure: Configuring rsync 2.5.5
....
$ make
...
lsbcc -g -O2 -DHAVE_CONFIG_H -Wall -W  -o rsync rsync.o \
generator.o receiver.o cleanup.o sender.o exclude.o util.o \
main.o checksum.o match.o syscall.o log.o backup.o options.o \
flist.o io.o compat.o hlink.o token.o uidlist.o socket.o \
fileio.o batch.o clientname.o params.o loadparm.o \
clientserver.o access.o connection.o authenticate.o \
lib/fnmatch.o lib/compat.o lib/snprintf.o lib/mdfour.o \
lib/permstring.o zlib/deflate.o zlib/infblock.o zlib/infcodes.o \
zlib/inffast.o zlib/inflate.o zlib/inftrees.o zlib/infutil.o \
zlib/trees.o zlib/zutil.o zlib/adler32.o  -lpopt -lresolv
authenticate.o(.text+0x83d): In function `auth_client':
authenticate.c:278: undefined reference to `getpass'
collect2: ld returned 1 exit status
make: *** [rsync] Error 1
```

13.5.2   Checking the Binary

The **lsbappchk** can be used to statically check a binary for LSB compliance (Example 13.14). The static application checker examines an application to check that it is using only the libraries, interfaces, and runtime loader specified by the LSB, as well as to verify that its program image has some features required by the ELF format.

Example 13.14: Running the Application Checker

```
$ lsbappchk rsync
lsbappchk for LSB Specification 2.0.0
Checking binary rsync
$
```

If any problems are found, they will be output to standard error and recorded in a journal file named `journal.binary_name`.

The **lsbdynchk** can be used at runtime to check a binary for compliance. The dynamic application checker examines the application parameters at runtime according to the specification.

Further testing, such as running the binary in the LSB Sample Implementation and running any functional verification tests for the application, should be done at this stage.

13.5.3   FHS Issues

The **lsbappchk** tool is not able to verify that an application is completely LSB-compliant. Some aspects, such as File Hierarchy Standard compliance, currently need to be checked manually. For example, by default **rsync** uses a configuration file `rsyncd.conf` that resides in `/etc`. But the FHS says configuration files should reside in `/etc/opt/package`. This can be achieved by applying the patch in Example 13.15.

Example 13.15: An rsync Patch to Obey the FHS Requirements

```
--- rsync-2.5.5/rsync.h 2002-03-25 00:29:43.000000000 -0700
+++ rsync-2.5.5.lsb/rsync.h 2003-05-13 18:25:25.000000000 -0600
@@ -26,7 +26,7 @@
 #define RSYNC_RSH_ENV "RSYNC_RSH"

 #define RSYNC_NAME "rsync"
-#define RSYNCD_CONF "/etc/rsyncd.conf"
+#define RSYNCD_CONF "/etc/opt/lsb-rsync/rsyncd.conf"

 #define DEFAULT_LOCK_FILE "/var/run/rsyncd.lock"
 #define URL_PREFIX "rsync://"
```

Similarly **rsync** can be configured to install into `/opt/lsb-rsync` instead of `/usr/local` by passing the `--prefix=/opt/lsb-rsync` parameter to the `configure` script.

13.5.4   Further Examples

Further examples of building LSB-compliant versions of applications can be found in the LSB Application Battery described in Chapter 14.

13.6   BUILDING THE LSB DEVELOPMENT ENVIRONMENT

Most of the source code for the lsb-build-base package is auto-generated from the LSB Written Specification database as illustrated in Figure 13.1. This has the benefit that the header files and stub libraries are synchronized with the specification. Normally it should not be necessary for people to build the source code from the database, though all of the scripts and the contents of the database are publically available in the LSB CVS repository.[4]

Source tarballs and source RPM packages for the lsb-build-base, lsb-build-cc, and lsb-build-chroot are available from the LSB FTP Archive.[5] The tarballs contains a readme that describes how to build the package and the source RPM packages can be built as usual with the **rpm** tool (Example 13.16).

Example 13.16: Building RPM Packages

```
# rpm --rebuild lsb-build-base-1.3.4-1.src.rpm
```

13.7   EXPANDING THE LSB DEVELOPMENT ENVIRONMENT

13.7.1   Using Compilers Other Than GCC

Nearly all of the testing and use of the LSB Development Environment has been with GCC as the compiler. It is possible to build LSB-compliant applications using other compilers.

Using the header files and stub libraries of the Development Environment is not strictly necessary, though it almost certainly will be easier to do so. The changes in the build process required to use another compiler can be summarized as follows.

• Use the LSB-compliant header files (lsb-build-base package).

---

4. http://gforge.freestandards.org/

5. ftp://ftp.freestandards.org/pub/lsbdev/released/source/

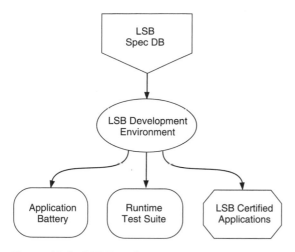

Figure 13.1: LSB Development Environment

- Use the LSB-compliant libraries. Using the Development Environment stub libraries has the advantage that link errors will occur if you attempt to use non-LSB interfaces.

- Ensure that the binary uses the LSB dynamic linker instead of the standard Linux linker for that architecture. For example, on x86 machines /lib/ld-lsb.so.1 should be used instead of /lib/ld-linux.so.2.

If you use lsb-build-chroot, then the first two changes are taken care of automatically. The way to achieve the third one will be compiler-dependent; as an example, with **gcc** this is done by editing the specs configuration file.

13.7.2   Integration with an IDE

Integration of lsb-build-cc with an IDE should be fairly straightforward, as the only change required is to call **lsbcc** instead of the normal compiler. In the case of lsb-build-chroot it would be necessary to run the compilation process inside of the chroot. This could be achieved using a helper program, or perhaps communicating with a compilation daemon that is running inside the chroot.

13.7.3   Using Non-LSB Interfaces

Sometimes developers are not able to build a completely LSB-compliant application as the core functionality of their program depends on a feature not included into the LSB Written Specification. However, for compatibility reasons, they still want to be as LSB-compliant as possible.

An example of this would be a dependence on a C library interface or a system call that is not in the LSB Written Specification. In this case it is not possible to simply supply a shared library with the application or to statically link the requirement to make the binary LSB-compliant. By modifying the LSB Development Environment, it is still possible to use it to build the binary and get the associated benefits. In the above case, the simplest approach would be to retrieve the source for the stub libraries, manually add the required interfaces, and build a new version of the stub libraries. Similarly, prototypes can be added to the LSB header files.

13.8   DOWNLOADING THE LSB DEVELOPMENT ENVIRONMENT

To obtain the LSB Development Environment go to the LSB Download Web page.[6] Table 13.2 represents the information that can be accessed via the World Wide Web.

lsb-build-base   The LSB Development Environment base package provides stub libraries and header files. These can be used to build LSB-compliant applications. Note that the version number of the package refers to the version of the specification that the stub libraries and header files have been generated for.

lsb-build-c++   This package provides interim C++ building support for the lsb-build packages. It adds C++ headers and LSB-conformant builds of the static C++ libraries to the files installed by lsb-build-base.

---

6. http://www.linuxbase.org/download/

Table 13.2: Development Environment Download Page

Specification Version	Package	Version	Architecture
2.0	`lsb-build-base`	2.0.0–1	I486, IA64, PPC, PPC64, S390, S390x, x86_64, SRC
2.0	`lsb-build-c++`	2.0.0–1	I486, IA64, PPC, PPC64, S390, S390x, x86_64, SRC
2.0	`lsb-build-cc`	2.0.0–1	I486, IA64, PPC, PPC64, S390, S390x, x86_64, SRC
2.0	`lsb-build-chroot`	2.0.0–1	I486, IA64, PPC, PPC64, S390, S390x, x86_64, SRC

`lsb-build-cc`   This package provides **lsbcc**, which is one of the approaches that can be used to build LSB-conformant applications.

`lsb-build-chroot`   The LSB Development Environment is a tool to make it easier to generate LSB-compliant binaries.

## CHAPTER FOURTEEN

Using
the Application Battery

The LSB Application Battery is a collection of several open source applications built to comply with the LSB Written Specification. The LSB project provides these applications to be used as further proof that a Linux distribution is able to support installation and execution of LSB-compliant applications.

Certification of a Linux distribution requires several methods to ensure compliance with the LSB Written Specification. The LSB Runtime test suite is used to test for the proper behavior of many of the system APIs. The LSB library checker verifies that all LSB-specified shared libraries and their respective APIs are present on the system. The third major test for compliance of a Linux distribution is the LSB Application Battery.

The choice of applications in the Battery is designed to exercise all of the LSB-specified shared libraries in a more real world situation. Using the Application Battery in this way complements the LSB Runtime test suite to provide a more thorough validation of a Linux distribution.

A further area where the Application Battery is useful is in its use of the LSB Development Environment. By using the Development Environment to build applications that use all of the LSB shared libraries, it helps to identify any deficiencies present in the header files and stub libraries of LSB Development Environment. Because the **lsbdev** is created directly from the data used in the Written Specification, it uncovers any problem with the specification itself.

Finally, beyond its use in testing Linux distributions and in validating **lsbdev** the Application Battery can be used to show application developers what steps are necessary to build a typical application to be compliant with the LSB.

Before going any further in discussing what the Application Battery (appbat) is and how it is used, it needs to be mentioned what appbat is not. The applications in appbat should not be considered for use in a production environment. Although building these applications for LSB compliance required minimal modifications from the upstream source, the LSB project has only performed minimal testing. The purpose of appbat is not to create production-ready substitutes for the same applications shipped with a Linux distribution. Instead, the applications in the Battery should only be used to test a Linux distribution for adherence to the LSB Written Specification.

14.1   UNDERSTANDING THE APPLICATION BATTERY

14.1.1   Common Open Source Applications

The LSB Application Battery is a collection of common open source applications that have been built using the LSB Development Environment to ensure they comply with the LSB Written Specification. In some instances, the application was simply recompiled to ensure the LSB dynamic linker is used instead of the system linker. A few of the applications have small patches applied to them to fix simple problems where the application was using a non-LSB argument type, or where a configure script produced wrong results when used with the **lsbdev**. For a few others, there are more significant patches. One example is the **rsync** application which uses the deprecated `getpass()` API. The patch for **rsync** replaces the use of `getpass()` with a call to `getpassword()`, a subroutine written specifically for the LSB version of **rsync** that provides the same return value as that expected from `getpass()`.

The choice of applications that comprise appbat was influenced by several factors. First of all, the applications needed to exercise as many of the LSB-defined shared libraries as possible. This was done to augment the testing already being done on the libraries by way of the LSB Runtime test suites. Another factor was the need to include applications that are open source and use a license allowing the LSB team to redistribute them along with the other test tools. To be considered for inclusion in appbat, an application also had to be fairly close to complete adherence to the LSB Written Specification. This means it could not use any non-LSB APIs from the LSB shared libraries, and only use a minimal number of non-LSB shared libraries.

For the initial LSB v1.2 Certification program, appbat only consisted of four applications, of which only two needed to be tested. When the LSB v1.3 Certification program began, the number of applications increased to eleven for the Intel 32-bit architecture, eight for the Itanium architecture, and ten for the PowerPC 32-bit architecture. An additional requirement for LSB v1.3 is that all LSB Certification Ready applications in appbat must be used when certifying an LSB Runtime Environment. An application is considered LSB Certification Ready when it has met all the requirements for LSB Application certification, including things like passing the LSB application checker, executing properly in the LSB Sample Implementation, and executing properly in two different LSB Certified Runtime Environments. Here is a list of the eleven applications in appbat for the LSB v2.0 Certification program for all supported processor architectures:

- Apache—Web server
- Celestia—visual space simulation
- **expect**—application that "talks" to other programs
- **groff**—document formatting system
- Lynx—text-based Web browser
- Python—interpreted, interactive, object-oriented programming language
- **rsync**—program for synchronizing files over a network
- Samba—file and print server for SMB/CIFS clients
- Tcl—embedded scripting language
- XPaint—paint program for the X Window System
- **xpdf**—PDF file viewer for the X Window System

14.1.2   Use of Application Battery in LSB Runtime Environment Certification

One step in testing a Linux runtime environment for compliance with the LSB Written Specification is to successfully execute the applications from the LSB Application Battery. By doing so, you demonstrate the ability of the runtime environment to install a set of LSB-compliant applications and prove the applications execute properly. Testing of the Application Battery adds further evidence that the LSB-defined APIs in the shared libraries of the runtime environment are supported correctly. The LSB Runtime test suites test the LSB APIs in isolated fashion. The Application Battery tests the APIs in a more practical fashion by using them as part of an actual application.

14.1.3   Caveats of Application Battery

As stated earlier, the applications in the Application Battery are open source applications that may be found on many Linux distributions. However, these applications should not be considered fit for use in a true production environment. The primary reason for this is the limited testing performed on these specially built versions. Most of the applications will behave identically to those already available on most Linux systems, but some of them had certain features disabled in order to make them LSB-compliant. The loss of these features will usually affect only the internal operation of the application. In a few instances, the application may perform slower because it could not take advantage of some non-standard code optimizations.

The LSB workgroup has been in contact with the upstream maintainers of many of the appbat applications. By demonstrating what is required to make these applications LSB-compliant, the LSB workgroup is helping the development teams to see how easy it is to adhere to the LSB Written Specification. Some of these open source projects have agreed to strive for LSB compliance. In some cases, they are accepting LSB-specific patches into their upstream source. Certain development teams are providing a location on their project Web sites where an LSB Certification Ready version of their application can be downloaded.

14.2   USING THE APPLICATION BATTERY FOR CERTIFICATION

14.2.1   Accessing the Application Battery

The applications of the LSB Application Battery are available for download from the Free Standards Group FTP site.[1] This directory contains several subdirectories containing applications for different versions of the LSB Written Specification, as well as a subdirectory containing prerelease versions of the applications. Official versions of the applications are in directories of the format `released-LSB_version`, where `LSB_version` is the applicable version of the LSB Written Specification. For example, the appbat applications for LSB v1.3 are in the directory `released-1.3.0`. The prerelease versions of the applications are in the `beta` directory.

Within each of the release directories and the `beta` directory there are subdirectories for each of the processor architectures supported by the particular version of the specification. Because the LSB v1.2 Written Specification was only available for the Intel 32-bit processor architecture, there are no subdirectories in the `released-1.2.0` directory. Separating the applications by processor type makes it easier to download all the applications needed for runtime environment certification in one go.

Example 14.1 is a brief snapshot of the directory structure on the FTP site to show how it is organized.

14.2.2   Installing the Application Battery

The installation of the appbat applications is the first step in using appbat for LSB certification of a Linux runtime environment. The distribution must prove that it can install an application packaged in the RPM package format as described in the LSB Written Specification. The installation can be performed using the **rpm** command itself or by using any other command capable of reading an RPM package. For example, on the Debian distribution, the **alien** command can be used to convert the RPM-packaged application to a `.deb` package. Once converted, the application can be installed with the **dpkg** command.

---

1. `ftp://ftp.freestandards.org/pub/lsb/app-battery/`

Example 14.1: Application Battery Directory Structure

```
pub ->
  lsb ->
    app-battery ->
      beta ->
        ia32 ->
        ia64 ->
        ppc32 ->
        ppc64 ->
        s390 ->
        s390x ->
        x86_64 ->
      released-1.2.0 ->
      released-1.3.0 ->
        ia32 ->
        ia64 ->
        ppc32 ->
        s390 ->
        s390x ->
      released-2.0.0 ->
        ia32 ->
        ia64 ->
        ppc32 ->
        ppc64 ->
        s390 ->
        s390x ->
        x86_64 ->
```

All of the applications in appbat have been packaged so that they require a package providing lsb-core-*arch*, where *arch* is the processor architecture, to already be installed on the system. If an attempt to install an appbat application is made without the required package being present, you will get an error message similar to the one shown in Example 14.2.

Example 14.2: Installation Error Message

```
$ rpm -ivh lsb-xpaint-2.7.0-1.lsb20.i486.rpm
error: Failed dependencies:
        lsb-core-ia32 >= 2.0 is needed by lsb-xpaint-2.7.0-1.lsb20
```

Every LSB Certified Runtime Environment must have a package installed that will provide the needed dependency for LSB-compliant applications. Furthermore, an LSB-compliant application must not rely on any commands or applications outside of those listed in the LSB Written Specification. This applies to installation of the application as well as to its normal operation.

When an LSB-compliant application is installed and tested on a full Linux distribution that is also an LSB Certified Runtime Environment, the application may perform properly even though it is using non-LSB commands. To help identify any potential problems, the application must also be tested in the LSB Sample Implementation. Because the Sample Implementation only has LSB-specified commands, it will cause the application to fail when it tries to make use of a non-LSB command. With the appbat applications being LSB-compliant, they have demonstrated that they only rely on LSB-specified commands.

14.2.3 Configuring the Application Battery

Some of the appbat applications will require a small amount of configuration before they can be used during LSB certification testing of a Linux runtime environment. Instructions for installing, configuring, and testing the applications are available on the LSB Web site at `http://www.linuxbase.org/ appbat/fvt-2.0.0/`. The instructions are divided into two sections. The first section covers the installation and setup of a particular application. The second section details the functional tests to be performed in order to validate correct execution of the application. Installation of the appbat applications was covered in the previous section of this chapter. All the appbat applications are installed in a similar fashion, so no further discussion is necessary. Instead, this section will describe some of the configuration steps performed on the applications.

Some of the configuration steps described in the Application Battery functional test pages are not really necessary on most Linux distributions. The items to be added or modified are already present on these systems even though they are not specified by the LSB. Still, the steps need to be verified to ensure the application can run on even a minimally compliant system, such as the LSB Sample Implementation. Two examples of such configuration steps are the addition of entries to the `/etc/services` file for **rsync** and Apache.

Both these applications have server components that run as system services, thus requiring appropriate **tcp** and **udp** entries in /etc/services. No additional configuration would need to be performed on Debian, Red Hat, or SuSE distributions because these entries would already exist. Conversely, these entries must be added on the LSB Sample Implementation in order to allow proper operation of the application service.

Another related example is the situation where the application must ensure that an entry for the nobody, nobody group, or both exist on the system. As with system services, the Apache and **rsync** application servers handle remote requests as the nobody user. The Tcl application also needs the nobody user when executing its suite of tests. Again, the LSB Sample Implementation will need extra configuration because the LSB only specifies the nobody user and group as optional.

In order to get some of the appbat applications operational, configuration files will need to be created or modified. In some instances, this will be the minimal configuration for the application, while in other instances the configuration is necessary for testing the application in such a way as to produce some well-known behavior. Configuring Samba involves either editing or creating the /etc/pam.d/samba configuration file to ensure Samba will use PAM for user authentication. To avoid conflicts with services already running on the host system, new configuration files must be created for both Samba and **rsync**. The Samba configuration file, /etc/opt/lsb/appbat/smb.conf, only has enough information in it to put the Samba server in the workgroup called WORKGROUP, share users' home directories on the system, and allow write access to the shared home directories. Similarly, the configuration file for **rsync**, /etc/opt/lsb/appbat/rsyncd.conf, sets up the **rsync** server to allow access to the /tmp/rsync directory and to enable write access to this directory.

Some of the applications in the Application Battery have server daemons that may conflict with those running on the host system. This can cause problems if two different daemons are both trying to service requests on the same port. To avoid this situation, the configuration instructions for Apache, **rsync**, and Samba tell the tester to stop appropriate daemons on the host before proceeding with the functional test. For the Apache Web server, any **httpd** or other daemons listening on the standard Web server port (80) must be stopped. With **rsync**, the tester must stop any **rsync** daemon currently running on the host system. Finally, the Samba **smbd** and **nmbd** server daemons must be stopped before attempting any functional tests.

The Samba application needs an additional bit of setup before it can be used to communicate with any SMB clients. Normally, when a connection is made from an SMB client to an SMB server, the authentication on the server is handled using the regular user IDs defined on the system. To avoid any confusion in the Samba functional tests that will be performed, the functional test configuration instructions tell the tester to create a user ID called smbuser and then to set its initial password to smb4lsb. Later, during testing the SMB client with the host system running the Samba server, this new user ID will be used for authentication.

For several appbat applications, some directories and files must be copied to expected locations to allow testing for some known results. The **rsync** application needs to have two directories created to act as the root directory for the files being shared by the **rsync** server and as a place to store files copied from the **rsync** server. To avoid conflicts with existing directories on the system, these new directories are placed in /tmp/rsync and /tmp/rsync.test. For both **rsync** and Samba some files will be copied to the respective server directories to ensure the file requested during the tests will exist. With the **expect**, Tcl, and **xpdf** applications, some files need to be downloaded from the Free Standards Group FTP site. The **expect** and Tcl applications have some automated tests that are part of the source code used to build them. The configuration instructions describe creation of directories to contain these tests and the process for populating them. The **xpdf** application instructs on downloading two PDF documents that will be used during functional testing.

There are a few additional configuration steps for several of the appbat applications, but they are much less involved. However, these steps will help you make testing of the applications go as smoothly as possible. For instance, the applications using X graphical interfaces (Celestia, XPaint, and **xpdf**) must make sure the DISPLAY environment variable is set properly. If it is not set correctly, it may affect their ability to execute and verify the functional tests. Another small configuration step is for the Python application. Part of the functional test for Python involves running some automated Python test scripts. Before the test, the tester is instructed to temporarily set aside the precompiled scripts that were created when building the Python application. Doing this will cause the test to compile the scripts before executing them.

14.2.4   Functional Testing of the Application Battery

As mentioned previously, the Application Battery is one of the components of certification for a Linux distribution. The distribution must prove it can install and execute applications that have demonstrated themselves to be compliant with the LSB Written Specification. The functional testing of the Application Battery is not overly exhaustive, but it will exercise enough of the applications to confirm they run properly on the Linux distribution. Some of the functional tests take advantage of automated regression tests that are provided with the source code for the application. The rest of the applications require a set of interactive steps to operate certain procedures in order to produce expected results. In most instances, it should not take more than a few hours to run through all the functional tests in the Application Battery.

In an ideal world, all applications in the Application Battery would have automated tests to verify their proper operation. Although the real world is far from ideal, at least some of the appbat applications provide regression tests. For the **expect** and Tcl applications, the test scripts must be downloaded from the Free Standards Group FTP site. The regression test scripts for Python are included with the package used to install the application. In each instance, the functional test for the application describes how to execute the regression test scripts and what the tests results should look like. The functional test for **expect** contains 25 tests, all of which must pass. The functional test for Tcl contains 6,851 tests, all of which must either pass or be skipped. For Python, there are more than 150 potential tests to be executed. The number of tests to pass may vary from system to system depending on what features are available, but none of them should fail.

The functional test for Celestia combines a few interactive steps with a more involved automated test. Unlike other automated tests, the one for Celestia does not produce any sort of log file nor does it report the numbers of tests passed and failed. Instead, the completion of the automated test is enough proof that the application operated successfully. The Celestia application is a graphic-intensive space simulator; its visual nature ensures that it stresses many of the graphical interfaces defined by the LSB Written Specification. The first few interactive steps in the functional test for Celestia involve entering the proper keys to have the application "travel" to the planets Earth and Mars. After this, the letter "d" is entered to run a demo scenario showing the features of Celestia. The scenario execution will take between five and ten minutes to complete.

The rest of the Application Battery functional tests are very interactive. With no formal regression tests available, the tests attempt to execute some of the more frequently used features of the applications. The **groff** application is part of a suite of text processing programs, but it does not provide a regression test and is mainly used via the command line. The LSB functional test for **groff** simply uses the application to format several manual pages provided with the application itself and display them on the screen. The Lynx application is a little more visual, being a text-based Web browser. Since the functional test for Lynx cannot assume that the system being tested is on a communications network, it restricts itself to displaying some simple Web pages that come with Lynx. By stepping through a few of these pages, it shows that Lynx is operating correctly.

Two more applications in the Application Battery are very visual in nature, so functional tests for them are more interactive and involve making sure the images displayed by the application are correct. The functional test for the XPaint application tries to verify correct operation for two of the main features of the application. First, the application is used to draw some simple shapes on the screen using a few of the color choices. Next, XPaint is used to take a snapshot of the screen and open it in a new window. The tester of XPaint just needs to make sure the application shows reasonable output. The functional test for **xpdf** has a file processing aspect to it in addition to the visual aspect. To facilitate testing **xpdf**, two PDF documents are downloaded from the Free Standards Group FTP site. The first test document is displayed by **xpdf** and the tester enters a few of the interactive commands. The second document is used to validate the text processing features of **xpdf**. It uses the **pdfinfo** command to display information contained in the PDF file, **pdftotext** to convert the PDF file into a text file, and **pdftops** to convert the PDF file into a PostScript file.

The final set of applications in the Application Battery are those that have a server feature. For these applications, there are interactive steps to start the server daemon and then perform tests to verify correct operation of the server. The functional test for Apache uses the Apache control script (**apachectl**) to start the Web server. To ensure the Web server is working, a browser is used to open the main Web page on the system being tested. The browser can be run on the same system if it is not connected to a network, or it can be run on a remote system. The browser is then used to display several Web pages on the server.

The testing for Samba and **rsync** is more involved because they each have a client side to them in addition to their server side. In the Samba functional test, the **smbd** and **nmbd** servers are started from the command line. After the servers have been started, the **smbclient** command is used to access the Samba server in several different ways. Testing for **rsync** is handled in a somewhat similar fashion. First, the **rsync** command is used to copy a file from one directory to another on the system. Next, **rsync** is started in daemon mode on the system. After the daemon is started, the **rsync** command is used to list the files being shared by the **rsync** daemon. A couple of files are then transferred to and from the **rsync** server to make sure this feature works.

14.3 CREATING THE APPLICATION BATTERY

14.3.1 Using LSB Development Environment

The applications in the Application Battery (Figure 14.1), just like any applications seeking to become LSB-certified, must adhere to the LSB Written Specification. The first issue to address is the requirement to only use the shared libraries specified by the LSB and only use the interfaces within those libraries that are specified by the LSB. The process to meet this requirement can be handled in multiple ways. The Application Battery uses the LSB Development Environment (**lsbdev**) to enforce the restrictions of the LSB at compile time. Using the header files and stub libraries from **lsbdev** helps to identify any non-compliant interfaces being used by the application. The **lsbcc** and **lsbc++** commands from **lsbdev** ensure that the application will search the **lsbdev**-provided headers and libraries before searching those on the system. This forces the application to link with the correct versions of any APIs

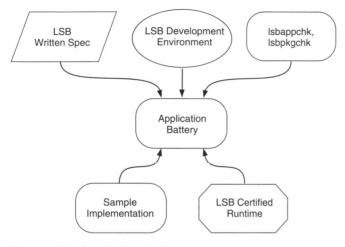

Figure 14.1: Application Battery

even though the shared libraries on the system may contain later versions of the same interface. Additionally, **lsbdev** causes the application to use the LSB dynamic linker instead of the default dynamic linker on the system. The **lsbcc** and **lsbc++** front end commands are designed to be used with any C or C++ compilers, but the Application Battery uses the GCC to build all the applications.

The LSB Written Specification for applications says that only LSB-specified shared libraries may be dynamically linked to the application. Any other library interfaces being used by the application can be accessed in one of two ways. First, the application can provide its own copies of any needed shared libraries and include them when installing the application itself. The other way to use non-LSB interfaces is to link them statically into the application. The choice of the way to proceed is up to the application's developer. For the LSB Application Battery there are examples of each method being used.

The Apache application in appbat includes three shared libraries built along with the application. Two of the libraries contain utility routines used by several different commands within Apache. The third shared library, **libexpat**, is built along with Apache because it is not a shared library defined by the LSB. Including a private version of **libexpat** makes sure the binary version of Apache has a known version of **libexpat** with which to work instead of relying on it being installed on the system where it will be executed. Counting on some expected behavior of a non-LSB shared library on a system is risky because the library's interfaces are not guaranteed to be consistent. To make sure the three shared libraries packaged along with Apache do not interfere with libraries installed on the system, they get installed in the same overall directory structure as the Apache application.

A few of the applications in appbat statically link some non-LSB libraries in order to meet the requirements of the LSB. For example, the XPaint application takes advantage of interfaces in the **libpng**, **libjpeg**, and **libtiff** libraries. Rather than build and package shared versions of these libraries to be shipped with XPaint, the Application Battery chose to link them in statically. To avoid being dependent on the version of the static library installed on the system where XPaint is built, appbat creates its own set of static libraries built from a known version of each one. This collection of libraries is known as the LSB Library Battery, or libbat. After the libbat is built, the static libraries are packaged together into an RPM package that is installed on top of the LSB Development Environment. The static libraries are placed in the same directory as the LSB stub libraries. Placing them there makes sure the appbat applications will link with the static versions of these libraries before finding whether the shared or static versions are installed on the system.

14.3.2   Resolution of Coding Problems

Building an application with the LSB Development Environment will help identify any compliance issues at compile time. This was true with many of the applications in the Application Battery and resulted in the need to resolve problems in the source code. Some of the changes were fairly simple, such as the need to use standard argument types instead of those not defined by the LSB. In other situations an application makes use of an interface that is not covered by the LSB but can be replaced by a similar function from the LSB. Rarely there are occasions where an application uses an interface with no equivalent function in the LSB. For this situation, the solution can involve incorporating the function into the application source code, disabling the portion of the application using the interface, or rewriting the application to handle the circumstances differently. A few examples from the Application

Battery demonstrate some of these coding problems and how they were overcome.

The Samba application had a few small issues with the upstream source code that kept it from building with the LSB Development Environment. One of the problems was something fairly simple where a variable was declared as the `uint` type. The `uint` type is usually defined in the header files of most Linux distributions, but it is not a standard type defined by the LSB. Most programmers use `uint` as shorthand instead of `unsigned short`. The solution to this problem was to add the capability to the configure script for Samba to detect whether or not the `uint` type was present in the Development Environment. When doing a non-LSB build `uint` will be found in the regular system headers and no changes will be seen in the Samba source code. The same configure script, when run in the LSB Development Environment, determines that `uint` has not been defined, so it adds a `#define uint unsigned short` to the `config.h` file included in all the Samba source code. The problem of using a non-LSB type definition can also be corrected by replacing all instances of the type by one of the types from the LSB.

The situation with **rsync** was a little more complicated than with Samba. The **rsync** application makes use of the `getpass()` function call to prompt for and read a password from the user running the command. Unfortunately, the `getpass()` interface is not defined by the LSB and no convenient equivalent exists either. For this situation, a function called `getpassword()` was added to the **rsync** source code. The algorithm of `getpassword()` was taken from the **glibc** documentation and was modified slightly to fulfill the needs of **rsync**. Next, the instance in the source code that called `getpass()` was changed to make a call to `getpassword()` instead. After that, **rsync** was able to avoid using a non-LSB interface but still got the desired results.

Another problem seen with **rsync**, as well as with some other applications, involved certain variables that were not handled correctly when the code was moved to a 64-bit Linux distribution. In many places, these applications declared variables to hold pointers, memory address offsets, or other items that have different sizes on 32-bit versus 64-bit operating systems. A variable to hold a pointer value would be defined as the type `int` because on 32-bit systems the size of an integer is the same as that of a pointer—32 bits. However, this coincidence does not hold true on 64-bit systems where the size of an integer and the size of a pointer are different. The answer to this problem is to change the definition of these variable types from `int` to `size_t`. The actual length of a `size_t` variable is dependent on whether the system is 32-bit or 64-bit. Changing the code in this way allowed **rsync** to have common code between the two different environments and to handle the different sizes of pointers correctly.

The Celestia application encountered a problem that was unique to a particular processor architecture. As part of building Celestia for LSB compliance, it is configured to use GL for its graphical operations instead of the non-LSB libraries like those provided with Gnome and KDE. Early in the startup code for Celestia running in GL mode, the program parses the command line for any arguments provided. It loops on the `getopt()` function call to retrieve arguments for as long as the return value from `getopt()` is greater than negative one. Unfortunately, the argument used to hold the return value was defined as `char` when the `getopt()` function is really returning an `int`. On most architectures supported by the LSB, the use of the wrong variable type causes no problems because the `char` type is signed by default. However, on the PowerPC architecture, the `char` type is unsigned. This means the return value from `getopt()` will never be less than negative one, so the program loops forever trying to read command-line parameters. To resolve this problem in the Application Battery, the source for Celestia was patched to change the argument type to `int`, thus allowing the program to proceed.

Another area where an application had to be changed involved some very old upstream source code. The XPaint application can read and write image files in several different formats, one of which is JPEG. The application has the capability by using function calls from the **libjpeg** shared library. As mentioned earlier, any non-LSB shared library must either be made available with the application, or the application must link the library statically. The Application Battery has implemented the second of these choices by statically linking **libjpeg** that is provided in the LSB Library Battery (libbat). As it turns out, the upstream source code for **libjpeg** is fairly old, so the configure script it uses to determine the type of hardware on which it is running is not aware of some of the newer hardware architectures, such as PPC64 and x86_64. The **libjpeg** library, like many other applications that try to do automatic configuration, uses a script called `config.guess` to figure out the processor architecture of the build system. The method used to get around this limitation was to replace the version of `config.guess` present in the **libjpeg** source code with a more current version. This update was done via a patch. After the patch is made, the configure script for **libjpeg** works correctly and allows XPaint to build successfully on all seven LSB processor architectures.

The previous several paragraphs give concrete examples of some coding problems that must be overcome when building an LSB-compliant application. Some of the problems were the same regardless of the processor being used, while others were only manifest on some of the architectures. Each application must be examined individually to see what difficulties exist, but the examples above should prove helpful in getting beyond any problems encountered.

14.3.3   Disabling Non-LSB Features

After resolving any coding problems in the application, such as those described in the previous section, there will still be some problems to overcome. Sometimes even the final choice of linking a static version of a function to the application will not work for various reasons. The application may use a shared library that cannot be linked statically to an application due to its software license. In other cases it can be difficult or even impossible to build a static version of some function needed by an application. For these situations, the only remaining options are to disable the part of the application using the shared library in question, or decide that the application is not a good candidate for meeting the LSB Written Specification. The LSB Application Battery encountered several situations like this and had to disable noncritical capabilities of the applications involved. This is another reason why it is important to understand that the applications in the LSB Application Battery cannot be considered production ready. A few examples of how this affected some applications should help to explain the problem as well as the solution.

The Apache Web server uses a database to manage user authentication. Since Apache has been designed to work on many different operating systems, it has a configure script that will determine the best available database engine to use. It can use several versions of the Berkeley DB (**libdb**), the GNU DB (**libgdbm**), or several other choices. This flexibility is very valuable, but it causes problems for building Apache in an LSB-compliant fashion. The LSB

Written Specification does not include any of the various database shared libraries, so another solution must be found. Fortunately, the Apache source code even considers this situation by providing its own limited database engine that can be built and shipped with Apache. The trick for building Apache in the Application Battery was to convince the configure script to use the internal database instead of relying on that found on the build system. The way this is accomplished is by providing the `--without-gdbm` and `--without-berkeley-db` flags when running configure. This prevents configure from searching on the build system for these non-LSB shared libraries. The configure script determines that it should use the internal shared library. To meet the requirement for non-LSB shared libraries, Apache provides the database library and two other utility libraries along with the Apache application during installation.

The situation with Celestia is similar to that for Apache in that it tries to use the best available shared libraries to handle the display of graphical information. Normally the application will utilize either GTK when running within a Gnome desktop environment or Qt when running within a KDE desktop environment. Neither of these graphic interface libraries is specified by the LSB, so another alternative must be found. Linking these interfaces statically to Celestia proved very difficult, so the Application Battery took a different direction. The source code for Celestia also contains support for using **libGL** for its graphics, which is good because **libGL** is a valid LSB shared library. Because the Application Battery is built on systems that most likely have either GTK, Qt, or both installed, the configure script for Celestia is called with the `--without-gtk` and `--without-kde` flags. This prevents configure from trying to use either GTK or Qt. Instead, Celestia gets built with support for only **libGL**, thus allowing it to comply with the LSB Written Specification.

The Samba application is another one designed to work in a variety of environments and take advantage of what is supported. One such feature is the use of the Common UNIX Printing System (CUPS) for print support. The CUPS interface provides a portability layer for the application and will work with whatever UNIX print system is supported, such as **lp** or **lpr**. This interface provides extra functionality beyond just submission of print jobs, so Samba exploits these capabilities. Once again, this is a problem for creating an LSB version of Samba since CUPS is not defined by the specification. The Application Battery instead uses the `--disable-cups` flag when calling configure to tell Samba to not attempt using the CUPS interfaces. Then Samba will fall back to the less functional **lp** or **lpr** command, but print support is still provided.

14.3.4   Alteration of Application Install Location

Once the applications in the Application Battery compile successfully, it is time to consider another requirement for LSB compliance. All applications must adhere to the Filesystem Hierarchy Standard (FHS) with regard to where the application is installed on a system. For the purposes of the Application Battery, all the applications included are considered third-party applications because they are not being shipped with the Linux distribution. The FHS specifies that third-party applications must install its component parts in certain directories. Any static portion of the application, such as the main application binary, must be installed under the `/opt` directory. Any configuration files associated with the application must be installed under the `/etc/opt` directory. Any files that can be modified while the application is running are to be installed under the `/var/opt` directory. The LSB Application Battery installs all of its applications under the `/opt/lsb/appbat`, `/etc/opt/lsb/appbat`, and `/var/opt/lsb/appbat` directories.

The method for modifying the install location for the Application Battery applications varied somewhat depending on how the application was written. Some of the more well-behaved applications use the `DESTDIR` variable in their makefiles for installation. This makes it easy to set `DESTDIR` to `/opt/lsb/appbat` and then use the application's regular makefile to install it. Unfortunately, not all applications are as considerate when it comes to alternative installation locations. For these situations, the Application Battery used other methods, such as patching a makefile to allow other install locations. The general solution for this kind of problem is going to involve a decision tree. The best scenario is when `DESTDIR` is supported. If it is not, then an examination of the application install code is necessary to determine how best to modify it.

14.4   DOWNLOADING THE APPLICATION BATTERY

To obtain the LSB Application Battery go to the LSB Download Web page.[2]
Table 14.1 represents the information that can be accessed via the World
Wide Web.

lsb-apache-2.0.49   LSB-conformant version of Apache, a powerful,
    full-featured, efficient, and freely available Web server. It is the most
    popular Web server on the Internet. Apache is added to the LSB
    Application Battery primarily to demonstrate networking, threads,
    and application-supplied shared libraries.

lsb-celestia-1.3.1   LSB-conformant version of Celestia, a free real-
    time space simulation that lets you experience our Universe in three
    dimensions. Celestia is added to the LSB Application Battery primarily
    to demonstrate a C++ program that uses the OpenGL library.

lsb-expect-5.41.0   LSB-conformant version of **expect**, a Tcl extension
    for automating and testing interactive applications such as **telnet**, **ftp**,
    passwd, **fsck**, **rlogin**, **tip**, and so on. This program is added to the LSB
    Application Battery primarily to demonstrate package dependencies,
    as it depends on LSB conforming Tcl. It is also used in building the
    LSB Runtime test suite.

lsb-groff-1.19   LSB-conformant version of **groff**, a document formatting
    system. It is added to the LSB Application Battery primarily to
    demonstrate the use of C++ programs.

lsb-lynx-2.8.5   LSB-conformant version of Lynx, a text-based Web
    browser. Lynx is added to the LSB Application Battery primarily to
    demonstrate the use of the **ncurses** library.

---

2. http://www.linuxbase.org/download/

Table 14.1: Application Battery Download Page

Specification Version	Package	Version	Architecture
2.0	`lsb-apache-2.0.49`	1.2.lsb20	I486, IA64, PPC, PPC64, S390, S390X, x86_64, SRC
2.0	`lsb-celestia-1.3.1`	1.2.lsb20	I486, IA64, PPC, PPC64, S390, S390X, x86_64, SRC
2.0	`lsb-expect-5.41.0`	1.2.lsb20	I486, IA64, PPC, PPC64, S390, S390X, x86_64, SRC
2.0	`lsb-groff-1.19`	1.2.lsb20	I486, IA64, PPC, PPC64, S390, S390X, x86_64, SRC
2.0	`lsb-lynx-2.8.5`	1.2.lsb20	I486, IA64, PPC, PPC64, S390, S390X, x86_64, SRC
2.0	`lsb-python-2.3.4`	1.2.lsb20	I486, IA64, PPC, PPC64, S390, S390X, x86_64, SRC
2.0	`lsb-rsync-2.6.2`	1.2.lsb20	I486, IA64, PPC, PPC64, S390, S390X, x86_64, SRC
2.0	`lsb-samba-3.0.4`	1.2.lsb20	I486, IA64, PPC, PPC64, S390, S390X, x86_64, SRC
2.0	`lsb-tcl-8.4.6`	1.2.lsb20	I486, IA64, PPC, PPC64, S390, S390X, x86_64, SRC
2.0	`lsb-xpaint-2.7.0`	1.2.lsb20	I486, IA64, PPC, PPC64, S390, S390X, x86_64, SRC
2.0	`lsb-xpdf-1.01`	1.2.lsb20	I486, IA64, PPC, PPC64, S390, S390X, x86_64, SRC

`lsb-python-2.3.4`   LSB-conformant version of Python, an interpreted, interactive, object-oriented programming language. It includes modules, classes, exceptions, very high-level dynamic data types, and dynamic typing. Python is added to the LSB Application Battery because the included test suite exercises many LSB features including sockets, networking, curses, and others.

`lsb-rsync-2.6.2`   LSB-conformant version of **rsync**, a program for bringing remote and host files into sync very quickly. It is fast because it just sends the differences in the files over the network instead of sending the complete files. Often, **rsync** is used as a very powerful mirroring process, or just as a more capable replacement for the **rcp** command. This program is added to the LSB Application Battery primarily to demonstrate the use of networking.

`lsb-samba-3.0.4`   LSB-conformant version of Samba, an SMB server that can be used to provide network services to SMB (sometimes called *LAN Manager*) clients. Samba uses NetBIOS over TCP/IP (NetBT) protocols and does *not* need the NetBEUI (Microsoft Raw NetBIOS frame) protocol. Samba is added to the LSB Application Battery primarily to demonstrate the use of networking and of PAM-based authentication.

`lsb-tcl-8.4.6`   LSB-conformant version of Tcl, a simple scripting language designed to be embedded in other applications. This package also includes **tclsh**, a simple example of a Tcl application. Tcl is added to the LSB Application Battery primarily because the included test suite exercises many LSB features; it also provides a dependency for the LSB-conformant version of expect.

`lsb-xpaint-2.7.0`   LSB-conformant version of XPaint, an X Window System color image editing and painting program. It is added to the LSB Application Battery primarily to demonstrate the use of X11 libraries.

`lsb-xpdf-1.01`   LSB-conformant version of **xpdf**, an X Window System viewer for Portable Document Format (PDF) files. This is a small and efficient program which uses standard X fonts. It is added to the LSB Application Battery primarily to demonstrate the use of C++ programs that exercise the X11 libraries.

GNU Free Documentation License

Version 1.1, March 2000

0 PREAMBLE

The purpose of this License is to make a manual, textbook, or other written
document "free" in the sense of freedom: to assure everyone the effective
freedom to copy and redistribute it, with or without modifying it, either
commercially or noncommercially. Secondarily, this License preserves for
the author and publisher a way to get credit for their work, while not being
considered responsible for modifications made by others.

This License is a kind of "copyleft," which means that derivative works of
the document must themselves be free in the same sense. It complements the
GNU General Public License, which is a copyleft license designed for free
software.

We have designed this License in order to use it for manuals for free software, because free software needs free documentation: A free program should

come with manuals providing the same freedoms that the software does. But this License is not limited to software manuals; it can be used for any textual work, regardless of subject matter or whether it is published as a printed book. We recommend this License principally for works whose purpose is instruction or reference.

1   APPLICABILITY AND DEFINITIONS

This License applies to any manual or other work that contains a notice placed by the copyright holder saying it can be distributed under the terms of this License. The "Document," below, refers to any such manual or work. Any member of the public is a licensee, and is addressed as "you."

A "Modified Version" of the Document means any work containing the Document or a portion of it, either copied verbatim, or with modifications and/or translated into another language.

A "Secondary Section" is a named appendix or a front-matter section of the Document that deals exclusively with the relationship of the publishers or authors of the Document to the Document's overall subject (or to related matters) and contains nothing that could fall directly within that overall subject. (For example, if the Document is in part a textbook of mathematics, a Secondary Section may not explain any mathematics.) The relationship could be a matter of historical connection with the subject or with related matters, or of legal, commercial, philosophical, ethical, or political position regarding them.

The "Invariant Sections" are certain Secondary Sections whose titles are designated, as being those of Invariant Sections, in the notice that says that the Document is released under this License.

The "Cover Texts" are certain short passages of text that are listed, as Front-Cover Texts or Back-Cover Texts, in the notice that says that the Document is released under this License.

A "Transparent" copy of the Document means a machine-readable copy, represented in a format whose specification is available to the general public, whose contents can be viewed and edited directly and straightforwardly with generic text editors or (for images composed of pixels) generic paint programs or (for drawings) some widely available drawing editor, and that is suitable for input to text formatters or for automatic translation to a variety of formats suitable for input to text formatters. A copy made in an otherwise Transparent file format whose markup has been designed to thwart or discourage subsequent modification by readers is not Transparent. A copy that is not "Transparent" is called "Opaque."

Examples of suitable formats for Transparent copies include plain ASCII without markup, Texinfo input format, LaTeX input format, SGML or XML using a publicly available DTD, and standard-conforming simple HTML designed for human modification. Opaque formats include PostScript, PDF, proprietary formats that can be read and edited only by proprietary word processors, SGML or XML for which the DTD and/or processing tools are not generally available, and the machine-generated HTML produced by some word processors for output purposes only.

The "Title Page" means, for a printed book, the title page itself, plus such following pages as are needed to hold, legibly, the material this License requires to appear in the title page. For works in formats which do not have any title page as such, "Title Page" means the text near the most prominent appearance of the work's title, preceding the beginning of the body of the text.

2   VERBATIM COPYING

You may copy and distribute the Document in any medium, either commercially or noncommercially, provided that this License, the copyright notices, and the license notice saying this License applies to the Document are reproduced in all copies, and that you add no other conditions whatsoever to those of this License. You may not use technical measures to obstruct or control the reading or further copying of the copies you make or distribute. However, you may accept compensation in exchange for copies. If you distribute a large enough number of copies you must also follow the conditions in Section 3.

You may also lend copies, under the same conditions stated above, and you may publicly display copies.

3   COPYING IN QUANTITY

If you publish printed copies of the Document numbering more than 100, and the Document's license notice requires Cover Texts, you must enclose the copies in covers that carry, clearly and legibly, all these Cover Texts: Front-Cover Texts on the front cover, and Back-Cover Texts on the back cover. Both covers must also clearly and legibly identify you as the publisher of these copies. The front cover must present the full title with all words of the title equally prominent and visible. You may add other material on the covers in addition. Copying with changes limited to the covers, as long as they preserve the title of the Document and satisfy these conditions, can be treated as verbatim copying in other respects.

If the required texts for either cover are too voluminous to fit legibly, you should put the first ones listed (as many as fit reasonably) on the actual cover, and continue the rest onto adjacent pages.

If you publish or distribute Opaque copies of the Document numbering more than 100, you must either include a machine-readable Transparent copy along with each Opaque copy, or state in or with each Opaque copy a publicly-accessible computer-network location containing a complete Transparent copy of the Document, free of added material, which the general network-using public has access to download anonymously at no charge using public-standard network protocols. If you use the latter option, you must take reasonably prudent steps, when you begin distribution of Opaque copies in quantity, to ensure that this Transparent copy will remain thus accessible at the stated location until at least one year after the last time you distribute an Opaque copy (directly or through your agents or retailers) of that edition to the public.

It is requested, but not required, that you contact the authors of the Document well before redistributing any large number of copies, to give them a chance to provide you with an updated version of the Document.

4   MODIFICATIONS

You may copy and distribute a Modified Version of the Document under the conditions of Sections 2 and 3 above, provided that you release the Modified

Version under precisely this License, with the Modified Version filling the role of the Document, thus licensing distribution and modification of the Modified Version to whoever possesses a copy of it. In addition, you must do these things in the Modified Version:

A. Use in the Title Page (and on the covers, if any) a title distinct from that of the Document, and from those of previous versions (which should, if there were any, be listed in the History section of the Document). You may use the same title as a previous version if the original publisher of that version gives permission.

B. List on the Title Page, as authors, one or more persons or entities responsible for authorship of the modifications in the Modified Version, together with at least five of the principal authors of the Document (all of its principal authors, if it has less than five).

C. State on the Title page the name of the publisher of the Modified Version, as the publisher.

D. Preserve all the copyright notices of the Document.

E. Add an appropriate copyright notice for your modifications adjacent to the other copyright notices.

F. Include, immediately after the copyright notices, a license notice giving the public permission to use the Modified Version under the terms of this License, in the form shown in the Addendum below.

G. Preserve in that license notice the full lists of Invariant Sections and required Cover Texts given in the Document's license notice.

H. Include an unaltered copy of this License.

I. Preserve the section entitled "History," and its title, and add to it an item stating at least the title, year, new authors, and publisher of the Modified Version as given on the Title Page. If there is no section entitled "History" in the Document, create one stating the title, year, authors, and publisher of the Document as given on its Title Page, then add an item describing the Modified Version as stated in the previous sentence.

J. Preserve the network location, if any, given in the Document for public access to a Transparent copy of the Document, and likewise the network locations given in the Document for previous versions it was based on.

These may be placed in the "History" section. You may omit a network location for a work that was published at least four years before the Document itself, or if the original publisher of the version it refers to gives permission.

K. In any section entitled "Acknowledgements" or "Dedications," preserve the section's title, and preserve in the section all the substance and tone of each of the contributor acknowledgements and/or dedications given therein.

L. Preserve all the Invariant Sections of the Document, unaltered in their text and in their titles. Section numbers or the equivalent are not considered part of the section titles.

M. Delete any section entitled "Endorsements." Such a section may not be included in the Modified Version.

N. Do not retitle any existing section as "Endorsements" or to conflict in title with any Invariant Section.

If the Modified Version includes new front-matter sections or appendices that qualify as Secondary Sections and contain no material copied from the Document, you may at your option designate some or all of these sections as invariant. To do this, add their titles to the list of Invariant Sections in the Modified Version's license notice. These titles must be distinct from any other section titles.

You may add a section entitled "Endorsements," provided it contains nothing but endorsements of your Modified Version by various parties—for example, statements of peer review or that the text has been approved by an organization as the authoritative definition of a standard.

You may add a passage of up to five words as a Front-Cover Text, and a passage of up to 25 words as a Back-Cover Text, to the end of the list of Cover Texts in the Modified Version. Only one passage of Front-Cover Text and one of Back-Cover Text may be added by (or through arrangements made by) any one entity. If the Document already includes a cover text for the same cover, previously added by you or by arrangement made by the same entity you are acting on behalf of, you may not add another; but you may replace the old one, on explicit permission from the previous publisher that added the old one.

The author(s) and publisher(s) of the Document do not by this License give permission to use their names for publicity for or to assert or imply endorsement of any Modified Version.

5 COMBINING DOCUMENTS

You may combine the Document with other documents released under this License, under the terms defined in Section 4 above for modified versions, provided that you include in the combination all of the Invariant Sections of all of the original documents, unmodified, and list them all as Invariant Sections of your combined work in its license notice.

The combined work need only contain one copy of this License, and multiple identical Invariant Sections may be replaced with a single copy. If there are multiple Invariant Sections with the same name but different contents, make the title of each such section unique by adding at the end of it, in parentheses, the name of the original author or publisher of that section if known, or else a unique number. Make the same adjustment to the section titles in the list of Invariant Sections in the license notice of the combined work.

In the combination, you must combine any sections entitled "History" in the various original documents, forming one section entitled "History"; likewise combine any sections entitled "Acknowledgements," and any sections entitled "Dedications." You must delete all sections entitled "Endorsements."

6 COLLECTIONS OF DOCUMENTS

You may make a collection consisting of the Document and other documents released under this License, and replace the individual copies of this License in the various documents with a single copy that is included in the collection, provided that you follow the rules of this License for verbatim copying of each of the documents in all other respects.

You may extract a single document from such a collection, and distribute it individually under this License, provided you insert a copy of this License into the extracted document, and follow this License in all other respects regarding verbatim copying of that document.

7   AGGREGATION WITH INDEPENDENT WORKS

A compilation of the Document or its derivatives with other separate and independent documents or works, in or on a volume of a storage or distribution medium, does not as a whole count as a Modified Version of the Document, provided no compilation copyright is claimed for the compilation. Such a compilation is called an "aggregate," and this License does not apply to the other self-contained works thus compiled with the Document, on account of their being thus compiled, if they are not themselves derivative works of the Document.

If the Cover Text requirement of Section 3 is applicable to these copies of the Document, then if the Document is less than one quarter of the entire aggregate, the Document's Cover Texts may be placed on covers that surround only the Document within the aggregate. Otherwise they must appear on covers around the whole aggregate.

8   TRANSLATION

Translation is considered a kind of modification, so you may distribute translations of the Document under the terms of Section 4. Replacing Invariant Sections with translations requires special permission from their copyright holders, but you may include translations of some or all Invariant Sections in addition to the original versions of these Invariant Sections. You may include a translation of this License provided that you also include the original English version of this License. In case of a disagreement between the translation and the original English version of this License, the original English version will prevail.

9 TERMINATION

You may not copy, modify, sublicense, or distribute the Document except as expressly provided for under this License. Any other attempt to copy, modify, sublicense or distribute the Document is void, and will automatically terminate your rights under this License. However, parties who have received copies, or rights, from you under this License will not have their licenses terminated so long as such parties remain in full compliance.

10 FUTURE REVISIONS OF THIS LICENSE

The Free Software Foundation may publish new, revised versions of the GNU Free Documentation License from time to time. Such new versions will be similar in spirit to the present version, but may differ in detail to address new problems or concerns. See `http://www.gnu.org/copyleft/`.

Each version of the License is given a distinguishing version number. If the Document specifies that a particular numbered version of this License "or any later version" applies to it, you have the option of following the terms and conditions either of that specified version or of any later version that has been published (not as a draft) by the Free Software Foundation. If the Document does not specify a version number of this License, you may choose any version ever published (not as a draft) by the Free Software Foundation.

11 HOW TO USE THIS LICENSE FOR YOUR DOCUMENTS

To use this License in a document you have written, include a copy of the License in the document and put the following copyright and license notices just after the title page:

> Copyright (c) YEAR YOUR NAME.
> Permission is granted to copy, distribute and/or modify this document under the terms of the GNU Free Documentation License, Version 1.1 or any later version published by the Free Software Foundation; with the Invariant Sections being LIST THEIR TITLES, with the Front-Cover Texts being LIST, and with the Back-Cover Texts being

LIST. A copy of the license is included in the section entitled "GNU Free Documentation License."

If you have no Invariant Sections, write "with no Invariant Sections" instead of saying which ones are invariant. If you have no Front-Cover Texts, write "no Front-Cover Texts" instead of "Front-Cover Texts being LIST"; likewise for Back-Cover Texts.

If your document contains nontrivial examples of program code, we recommend releasing these examples in parallel under your choice of free software license, such as the GNU General Public License, to permit their use in free software.

Resources

B.1 Glossary

Applicant   The supplier who is in the process of having a product certified.

Certification   The proof of compliance by some agreed measure. Sometimes there is not a total proof, but a warranty. Additionally, there may be a logo or mark that can be used in association with a certified product.

Certification Agreement   The agreement between the applicant and the Certification Authority, which defines the certification service and contains the legal commitment by the applicant to the conditions of the certification service.

Certification Authority   The organization officially sanctioned by the Free Standards Group to manage the day-to-day operations of the LSB Certification program.

Certification Register   A record of all certified products, which is maintained by the Certification Authority and made publicly available via the Internet.

Certification System Deficiency   An agreed error in the certification system, which is inhibiting the certification process. The certification system includes both the certification process and information systems provided to implement certification. A Certification System Deficiency is one possible outcome of a problem report.

Certified Product   A product or product family that has successfully completed the certification process and for which the supplier of such product or product family has been notified in writing by the Certification Authority that certification has been achieved.

Compliance   A claim of conformance.

Conformance   Requirements are stated in a specification. They are an agreed set of rules defining what it means to meet the specification.

Conformance Requirements   A definition of the mandatory requirements a product must meet and any options it must implement in order to be considered conformant.

Conformance Statement   The documented set of claims describing precisely the way in which a product meets the conformance requirements, including which optional features are supported. It provides a precise identification of the certified product for which conformance is guaranteed. It also includes details on the specific configuration used to validate conformance, in sufficient detail to enable the results of any applicable tests to be reproduced.

Free Standards Group, The   A nonprofit corporation organized to accelerate the use and acceptance of open source technologies through the development, application, and promotion of standards.

Interpretation   Decision made by the Specification Authority that elaborates or refines the meaning of a Free Standards Group specification or a standard or specification referenced by a Free Standards Group specification. An Interpretation is one possible outcome of a problem report.

LSB   Linux Standard Base. This is a historical name, and does not limit the LSB Written Specification to any specific operating system.

LSB Application   LSB Application certification is for applications conforming to the LSB Written Specification. LSB Applications are the consumers of the services provided by LSB Runtime Environments.

LSB Development Environment   LSB Development Environment certification is for platforms on which LSB-conformant applications can be built from source code. Platforms providing an LSB Development Environment need not provide an LSB Runtime Environment.

LSB Internationalized Runtime Environment   LSB Internationalized Runtime Environment certification is for platforms providing services that conform to the LSB and OpenI18N specifications. The platform must be registered as conformant to the LSB Runtime Environment product standard prior to or concurrent with an LSB Internationalized Runtime Environment Product Standard registration.

LSB Runtime Environment   LSB Runtime Environment certification is for platforms providing services that conform to the LSB Written Specification.

OpenI18N   The Free Standards Group Open Internationalization Initiative. This was formerly known as the LI18NUX specification.

Platform   An operating system environment. It may consist of a complete operating system with kernel, libraries, and utilities; it may also be a hosted environment or emulation that provides the equivalent functionality.

Problem Report   A question of clarification, intent, or correctness of the specification(s), test suites, or certification system, which, if accepted by the Specification Authority, will be resolved into an Interpretation, Test Suite Deficiency, or Certification System Deficiency, respectively.

Product Standard   The document in which conformance requirements are specified for a particular type of product, and against which products may be certified in the program. There will be one product standard for each type of product to be certified, that is, one for LSB Runtime Environment, LSB Application, LSB Development Environment, and LSB Internationalized Runtime Environment, respectively. Apart from the LSB Internationalized Runtime Environment product standard, there will be a set of such product standards for each architecture specified by the LSB Written Specification.

Registration Form   A form completed by the applicant to apply for certification for a particular product. The form contains information on the applicant and the product to be certified.

Specification Authority   A Free Standards Group workgroup, which is responsible for developing, maintaining, and interpreting the applicable Free Standards Group specification(s).

Supplier   A product vendor who is interested in, is applying for certification in, or has certified a product in the Free Standards Group certification program. During the period in which a supplier is going through the certification process to get a product certified, the supplier is referred to as an applicant.

Test Suite Deficiency   An agreed error in a test suite, which is causing it to produce an incorrect result code that impacts certification. A Test Suite Deficiency is one possible outcome of a problem report.

Test Suite Maintenance Authority   The organization(s) sanctioned by the Free Standards Group to maintain the test suites.

Trademark License Agreement   The agreement between the supplier and the Free Standards Group, which contains the legal commitment by the supplier to the conditions of use of the Free Standards Group trademark and the Free Standards Group certification program.

B.2   SUGGESTED READING

B.2.1   Books

- Kerninghan, Brian and Ritchie, Dennis. *The C Programming Language.* 2nd edition, Prentice Hall, 1988.

- Molay, Bruce. *Understanding UNIX/LINUX Programming: A Guide to Theory and Practice.* Prentice Hall, 2002.

- Newham, Cameron and Rosenblatt, Bill. *Learning the bash Shell.* 2nd edition, O'Reilly, 1998.

- Oram, Andy and Loukides, Mike. *Programming with GNU Software.* 1st edition, O'Reilly, 1995.

- Oualline, Steve. *Practical C Programming.* 3rd edition, O'Reilly, 1997.

- Robbins, Kay and Robbins, Steven. *Practical UNIX Programming.* 3rd edition, O'Reilly, 1995.

B.2.2 Articles

- Anderson, Stuart. "How to Build LSB Applications." *Linux Journal* 121, May 2004.

- "GNU gettext Utilities." GNU Translation Project, Free Software Foundation, 2002.

- McNeil, Scott. "Linux Distributions Agree on Standards." *Linux Journal* 108, April 2003.

B.2.3 Specifications

- *Sys V Application Binary Interface, MIPS RISC Supplement.* 3rd edition, The Santa Cruz Operation, IEEE Computer Society, 1990–1996.

- *IEEE Std 1003.1–2001 (POSIX).* Austin Group, IEEE Computer Society, The OpenGroup, 2001.

- *64-bit PowerPC ELF Application Binary Interface Supplement 1.7.* Ian Taylor, IBM, Free Standards Group, 1999, 2003.

B.3 BIBLIOGRAPHY

B.3.1 Books

- Bailey, Edward. *Maximum RPM.* SAMS Publishing, 1997.

- Corbet, Jonathan. *What Does It Mean to Signal Everybody?* Linux Weekly News, 2001.

B.3.2   Articles

- Kraft, George, IV. "Where to Install My Products on Linux?" *Linux Journal*, 2000.

B.3.3   Specifications

- *Linux Standard Base Specification 2.0*, The LSB Workgroup, Free Standards Group, 2003.

- *LSB 2.0 for the EAS/390 Architecture*, The LSB Workgroup, Free Standards Group, 2003.

- *LSB 2.0 for the IA32 Architecture*, The LSB Workgroup, Free Standards Group, 2003.

- *LSB 2.0 for the Itanium Architecture*, The LSB Workgroup, Free Standards Group, 2003.

- *LSB 2.0 for the Optheron Architecture*, The LSB Workgroup, Free Standards Group, 2003.

- *LSB 2.0 for the PowerPC Architecture*, The LSB Workgroup, Free Standards Group, 2003.

- *LSB 2.0 for the PPC64 Architecture*, The LSB Workgroup, Free Standards Group, 2003.

- *LSB 2.0 for the z/Architecture*, The LSB Workgroup, Free Standards Group, 2003.

B.3.4   Web Pages

- About Red Hat (`http://www.redhat.com/about/`)

- Application Battery (`http://www.linuxbase.org/appbat/`)

- Austin Group, The (`http://www.opengroup.org/austin/`)

- C User's Guide (`http://docs.sun.com/db/doc/817-5064/`)

- C++ User's Guide (`http://docs.sun.com/db/doc/817-5070/`)

- Conformance Statement Questionnaires (`http://www.opengroup.org/lsb/cert/docs/conformance.html`)

- Developing LSB-Certified Applications (http://www.ibm.com/developerworks/linux/library/l-lsb.html)
- DistroWatch.com (http://www.distrowatch.org/)
- Filesystem Hierarchy Standard (http://www.pathname.com/fhs/)
- Free Software Directory (http://www.gnu.org/directory/GNU/)
- Free Standards Group (http://www.freestandards.org/)
- Freeware for Solaris (http://www.sunfreeware.com/)
- FSG Certification (http://www.freestandards.org/certification)
- FSG GForge (http://gforge.freestandards.org/)
- GNU make (http://www.gnu.org/software/make/manual/make.html)
- Guide to LSB Certification (http://www.opengroup.org/lsb/cert/docs/LSB_Certification_Guide.html)
- IBM Copyright and Trademark Information (http://www.ibm.com/legal/copytrade.shtml)
- Java API (http://java.sun.com/reference/api/index.html)
- JNI Overview (http://java.sun.com/docs/books/tutorial/native1.1/concepts/index.html)
- Knopper.Net (http://www.knopper.net/)
- Linux Assigned Names And Numbers Authority, The (http://www.lanana.org/)
- Linux Defeats Microsoft Windows in Top 5 (http://www.reallylinux.com/docs/linwin.html)
- Linux From Scratch (http://www.linuxfromscratch.org/)
- Linux Kernel (http://lwn.net/2001/1220/kernel.php3)
- Linux Online: Distributions and FTP Sites (http://www.linux.org/dist/)
- LSB Bugzilla (http://bugs.linuxbase.org/)
- LSB Certification (http://www.opengroup.org/lsb/cert/)

- LSB Certification: Fee Schedule (`http://www.opengroup.org/lsb/cert/docs/LSB_Fee_Schedule.html`)

- LSB Certification: Frequently Asked Questions (`http://www.opengroup.org/lsb/cert/docs/faq.html`)

- LSB Certification: Problem Reporting and Interpretations System (`http://www.opengroup.org/lsb/cert/PR/`)

- LSB Certification Policy (`http://www.opengroup.org/lsb/cert/docs/LSB_Certification_Policy.html`)

- LSB Certification Register (`http://www.opengroup.org/lsb/cert/register.html`)

- LSB Development Environment (`http://www.linuxbase.org/build/`)

- LSB Futures Candidates (`http://www.linuxbase.org/futures/candidates/`)

- LSB Futures Selection Criteria (`http://www.linuxbase.org/futures/criteria/`)

- LSB Product Standards (`http://www.opengroup.org/lsb/cert/docs/prodstandards.html`)

- LSB Project Downloads (`http://www.linuxbase.org/download/`)

- LSB Project Proposal and Call for Participation (`http://old.lwn.net/1998/0528/a/lsb.html`)

- LSB Test Suites (`http://www.opengroup.org/lsb/cert/docs/testsuites.html`)

- LSB Written Specification (`http://www.linuxbase.org/spec/`)

- Managing Projects with make (`http://www.oreilly.com/catalog/make2/`)

- Open Group, The (`http://www.opengroup.org/`)

- Open Brand—Test Suite Acceptance Criteria, The (`http://www.opengroup.org/openbrand/testing/testprocs/accprocs.html`)

- Open Internationalization (`http://www.openi18n.org/`)

- PASC (`http://www.pasc.org/`)

- RPM Package Manager (http://www.rpm.org/)
- Rsync (http://rsync.samba.org/)
- Sample Implementation Download (http://ftp.freestandards.org/pub/lsb/impl/)
- Single UNIX Specification (http://www.unix.org/version3/)
- Sleepycat Software: Berkeley Database (http://www.sleepycat.com/)
- Solaris-compatible Thread Library (http://sourceforge.net/projects/sctl/)
- Study Shows Broad Use of Linux (http://www.eweek.com/print_article/0,3668,a=43824,00.asp)
- System V Application Binary Interface Group (http://www.caldera.com/developers/gabi/2003-12-17/contents.html)
- Technical Guide for Porting Applications from Solaris to Linux (http://www.ibm.com/developerworks/eserver/articles/porting_linux/)
- TET 3.3 Documentation (http://tetworks.opengroup.org/documents/docs33.html)
- TETware User Guide (http://tetworks.opengroup.org/documents/ 3.3/uguide.pdf)
- UNIX System, The (http://www.unix-systems.org/)
- Using and Porting the GNU Compiler Collection (GCC) (http://gcc.gnu.org/onlinedocs/gcc-2.95.2/gcc_toc.html)
- What is Copyleft? (http://www.gnu.org/copyleft/)

Book Logistics

C.1   READ ONLINE

The current version of this book can be found online in HTML (`http://lsbbook.gforge.freestandards.org/`) and PDF (`http://lsbbook.gforge.freestandards.org/lsb-book.pdf`) formats.

C.2   REPORT BUGS

The LSB accepts problem reports and suggestions via Bugzilla (`http://bugs.linuxbase.org/`).

C.3   OBTAIN SOURCE

This book is licensed under the GNU Free Documentation License, and its source is available online via CVS:

```
CVSROOT=:pserver:anonymous@cvs.gforge.freestandards.org:\
/cvsroot/lsbbook
cvs -d$CVSROOT login
cvs -d$CVSROOT -z3 co lsbbook
```

Index

Bold pages indicate significant topic coverage.

W

`waitpid()`, 35–36
`WARNING` result code, 135
`WCONTINUED` environment variable, 35
Web certification system, *see* LSB
      Certification, Web site
Wichmann, Mats, xxvi
`WIFCONTINUED` environment variable, 35
wrapper scripts, 49

X

X Server, 159
X Window System, 123, 195, 214
   test suite, *see* `lsb-test-vsw4`
X/Open Company Portability Guides, *see*
      XPGs
X11 libraries, 214
x86_64 architecture, 208
XDR (External Data Representation)
      ordering, 59
XFree86 project, xxi
xinetd, 160
XPaint, 195
   configuring, 201
   LSB-compliant version of, 208, 214
   shared libraries in, 206
   testing, 203
xpdf, 195
   configuring, 201
   LSB-compliant version of, 214
   testing, 203
XPGs (X/Open Company Portability
      Guides), 21

Y

Yeoh, Christopher, xxvi

Z

z/Architecture, 11